LOTUS 1-2-3
FOR WINDOWS

version 4

PRISMA Computer Courses are structured, practical guides to mastering the most popular computer programs. PRISMA books are course books, giving step-by-step instructions, which take the user through basic skills to advanced functions in easy to follow, manageable stages.

Now available:

dBase IV
Excel 4.0 for Windows
Lotus 1-2-3
MS-DOS
Novell Netware
UNIX
Windows
WordPerfect
WordPerfect for Windows

Ernst Tiemeijer

LOTUS 1-2-3 FOR WINDOWS

version 4

PRISMA COMPUTER COURSE

Prisma Computer Courses first published in Great Britain 1993 by

Het Spectrum
P.O. Box 2996
London N5 2TA London

Translation: George Hall
Production: LINE UP text productions

PRINTED IN THE EEC

British Library Cataloguing-in-Publication Data.
A catalogue record for this book is available from the British Library.

Contents

Foreword

No other software package has achieved world-wide distribution to an extent comparable to Lotus 1-2-3. Throughout the entire world there are twenty million users, making it, in fact, the industry standard. The numerous functions and the straightforward operation have resulted in this program constantly occupying a leading position according to sales and marketing statistics.

Due to immense technical developments in the areas of hardware and operating systems, there are various versions of Lotus 1-2-3 currently on the market: for DOS, OS/2, UNIX, Apple Macintosh and Windows.

This book deals with the version for Windows. *Lotus 1-2-3 Version 4 for Windows* provides all the features of the current DOS version and, in addition, the ease of operation and display options of the graphic user interface. Moreover, there are special facilities to enable data exchange with other applications running under Windows.

The Lotus 1-2-3 Version 4 for Windows (here abbreviated to 1-2-3/W) is designed for users who:

- have a powerful computer
- require a powerful spreadsheet
- make severe demands on data exchange facilities with other applications.

1-2-3 /W is also available in this form for the OS/2 operating system. If you are running the program under OS/2, this book will supply a great deal of useful information.

In 1-2-3 /W, three essential elements of classical PC software have been combined: spreadsheets, charts and database management. Working with 'electronic worksheets', spreadsheets, is the central point in

1-2-3/W. Using these, it is possible to gather together and edit all kinds of figures and calculations, also in three-dimensional form. In order to present the numerical data in a clear and sophisticated manner, the integrated graphic module is one of the components of the package. In addition, it is possible to manage data files systematically and to use these in the processing.

Using concrete examples, we shall outline the fundamental aspects of the instructions and functions of 1-2-3 /W in an explicit and systematic way, step by step. Important schemes are documented in checklists, allowing easy reference to problematic aspects, if any.

All the examples have been developed and tested on an IBM compatible computer. The names of the keys correspond to those on a standard IBM keyboard.

Ernst Tiemeyer, 1993

1   First steps with 1-2-3/W

Before being able to make optimal use of all the possibilities offered by Lotus, you must first become familiar with the fundamental concept of the program. This concerns knowledge of the application possibilities and the manner in which instructions are given.

1.1   Configuration criteria and areas of operation

1-2-3/W is an integrated program for the personal computer, providing a broad spectrum of possibilities. Spreadsheets are the focal point of the program. In addition, the package enables you to construct diagrams and to formulate systematic data management.

Under MS-DOS, Lotus 1-2-3 is the world-wide market leader. The new Windows version satisfies the operating ease demanded nowadays. At the same time, all special facilities provided by Windows, such as dynamic data exchange, are also available.

In order to be able to run the Windows version, you require a powerful PC in the following configuration:

a) Hardware requirements:

- A personal computer (PC) with an Intel processor of 80286 or higher; 80486 or 80586 are preferable.
- Sufficient internal memory - 4 Mb if you are running under Windows 3.x.
- A harddisk with a large capacity, or a server. Installation on a harddisk requires 13 Mb.
- A floppy diskdrive.
- Suitable input devices. In addition to using the keyboard to enter data and give commands, an indica-

tion device (normally a mouse) is both desirable and necessary for many functions and aspects.
■ Suitable output devices. Laser printers are supported by various fonts to reproduce the worksheets and diagrams on paper.

b) An operating system, extended if necessary:

■ The MS-DOS (from version 3.3 onwards) or DR-DOS operating system in combination with the Windows 3.x user interface. The Windows 3.1 version has distinct advantages compared to Windows 3.0.

1-2-3/W has three function areas which are operated identically:

1) Spreadsheets

The heart of the program. A spreadsheet is an electronic worksheet in which a large number of calculations can be made quickly. If there is any alteration in figures, the dependent results are recalculated. Special functions are:

■ a three-dimensional spreadsheet in which various worksheets can be organized in cne file;
■ many facilities to reproduce a table (*spreadsheet publishing*);
■ easy data exchange, both dynamic and static, between various tables.

2) Charts

Recorded figures and data can be displayed in orderly charts and diagrams for further processing or documentation. Available types are: line charts, bar charts in simple or stacked form, pie charts, XY charts, scatter charts and charts combining bars and lines. Three-dimensional chart display is also possible.

In order to bring a personal touch to these charts and diagrams, it is possible to make use of the many layout facilities, including labels and titles, scaling, colours and shading.

In addition to the facility of printing charts and diagrams on the printer or displaying them on the full screen, it is also possible to display a separate diagram window on the screen alongside the worksheet. The worksheet and the diagram can then be viewed simultaneously. Each alteration in the worksheet is then immediately processed and shown in the corresponding diagram.

3) Database

This enables information to be stored in a structured way and selected or sorted in the light of certain criteria.

These three components are not separate from each other - exchange of data is possible.

Separate utility programs are available to allow the integration of other applications:

- The *1-2-3 Translate* utility program enables you to exchange data with other spreadsheet programs and with the widely-used dBASE database program.
- The *DataLens* database driver enables you to work with dBASE IV files directly from 1-2-3/W, and also with databases such as Paradox and SQL-Server.

1.2 Installation

Installation of the program is necessary if you are going to work with 1-2-3/W for the first time. During installation, the program will be adjusted to the demands of your hardware.

Before beginning the installation, have all the program diskettes ready in front of you. There are five diskettes for a system with 3.5 inch drives. These diskettes contain the files which are necessary to install the program in addition to the actual program files. There is also a sixth diskette containing the so-called Adobe Type Managers (ATM). This supports the creation of sharp, clear-cut fonts in PostScript format.

Tip: Never use the original diskettes to install a program. Make copies of these diskettes first and then use the copies to install the program. Write-protect the original diskettes prior to copying by opening the small sleeve in 3.5" diskettes or by taping over the small notch in 5.25" diskettes. Then copy the diskettes using the *Copy Disk* option from the *Disk* menu of the File Manager under Windows. Apply labels to the copy diskettes corresponding to those of the originals.

Now the actual installation of 1-2-3/W can begin. Insert diskette 1 in drive A: Proceed as follows:

1. Start up Windows, if necessary, by typing WIN behind the DOS prompt and press Enter.
2. Activate the *File* menu in the Program Manager (using Alt-F or the mouse) and select the *Run* option.
3. Give the command to install by typing A:INSTALL in the text box.
4. Press Enter to confirm the command.

The installation program then copies all data to the hard-disk and then requests the company name. You can select one of four options from the subsequent screen:

■ Install 1-2-3
■ Install on a server
■ View product updates
■ Choose country driver and sort order

Select the first option by clicking on the first icon. This begins the installation of the program. Subsequently, you can select one of the three options dealing with the type of installation.

a) Default Install
b) Customized Install
c) Install for laptops.

The second option enables you to determine which extra options and functions you wish to install. The first option does not permit this.

The further installation procedure depends on your choice.

In all cases a dialog window appears in which you can specify the directory and drive on the harddisk where the program is to be installed. The default setting is the program directory C:\123R4W. If you adopt this proposal and the directory does not yet exist, the program will create the directory. Then the files are copied from the diskettes to this directory.

You can follow the progress on the screen. When necessary, you will be requested to insert the appropriate diskette in the relevant drive and to confirm the continuation by pressing Enter.

When all the files have been copied, a message to this effect will be shown on the screen. Only the necessary files are transferred to the harddisk, which may explain why not all diskettes have been used.

A new group window, *Lotus Applications*, is automatically created during the installation. This window contains the icons which belong to the newly-installed applications and, if present, icons belonging to other Lotus applications.

The most important icons have the following significance:

a) The *Lotus 1-2-3 Release 4* icon represents the program itself. This is used to start up the program.

b) The *1-2-3 Install* icon enables you to make modifications to the program installation later.

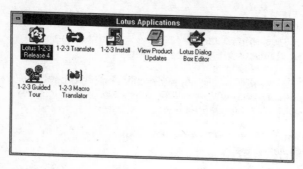

Group window for Lotus applications

As soon as the installation has ended you can begin work.

1.3   Starting up 1-2-3/W

There are various ways of starting up the 1-2-3/W program. In all cases, Windows must be running. Then proceed as follows:

a) **Starting up via the Program Manager:**

Click on the group window containing the 1-2-3/W icon and then double-click on the icon itself to activate the program. Double-click means pressing the left-hand mouse button twice in rapid succession.

You can also use the keyboard: Open the *Window* menu (Alt-W). Select *Lotus Applications* using the cursor keys or type the number in front of the option. Select the program in the *Lotus Applications* window using the cursor keys and press Enter to start it up.

b) **Starting up via the File Manager:**

Activate the *Main* group window (Alt-W, select Main). Select *File Manager* using the cursor keys and press Enter. Select the 123r4w directory from the appropriate drive (click on it using the mouse or go to it using the cursor keys) and press Enter. Then select *Pro-*

grams using Tab and the cursor keys or the mouse. Press Enter. Go to *123w.exe* using the cursor keys or the mouse and press Enter.

The title screen will appear briefly and the program will move on to display the first empty worksheet. You can now enter data to create your first file.

1.4   Operating principles

If you are going to work with 1-2-3/W for the first time, you will have to become familiar with the operating principles. To do this, we shall examine the initial screen a little more closely.

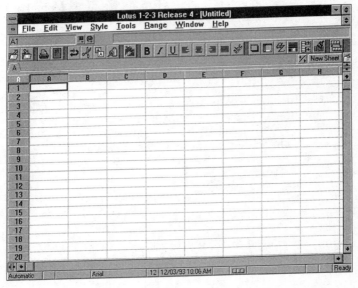

Opening screen with empty worksheet

a) Title bar

The name of the current worksheet is shown between square brackets behind the name of the program Lotus 1-2-3 Release 4. If no name has been specified as yet, 'Untitled' is displayed here in the meantime. At the extreme right- and left-hand sides of the title bar, small symbols are shown. The symbol in the upper left-hand corner (the Control menu button) enables you to open a menu dealing with certain window functions, such as closing, enlarging (maximizing), reducing (minimizing) and moving the window. By clicking on the symbols in the upper right-hand corner you can alter the size of the window immediately.

When one of the menus is chosen from the Menu bar, the Title bar becomes an Information bar, displaying information about the current processes and layout.

b) Menu bar

The names of the menus which are currently available are shown on the menu bar under the title bar. These form the basis for the execution of commands. The following menus are located on the menu bar:

- File
- Edit
- View
- Style
- Tools
- Range/Chart/Query
- Window
- Help

These are referred to as *pull-down menus* which are opened by clicking on them or by means of certain key combinations (Alt-underlined letter).

At the left-hand side of the menu bar, there is the window Control Menu button which enables you to specify the size and position of the worksheet window. This is activated by clicking on it or by means of the key combination Alt-hyphen. The menu is removed again by clicking outside it or by pressing the Alt key.

The symbol shown at the right-hand side of the menu bar is the same as that shown on the title bar, enabling you to alter the size of the worksheet window. If you click on this symbol, the window receives its own title bar containing the file name which simultaneously disappears from the application title bar. Only the name of the program is then shown there. Minimizing this window (down symbol) turns it into an icon (double-click to restore); maximizing it restores the original situation.

Note: For those who are already acquainted with the common Lotus 1-2-3 programs, the 'classic' Lotus menu can be displayed by pressing the slash (/) key. In that case, the upper line shows the menus available, the lower line indicates the options which can be selected from these menus.

c) The Edit line

This shows the contents of the cells. Data are entered and altered in the cells via this line. At the extreme left of this line, there is the selection indicator which displays the area of the worksheet which is currently selected. Next to this are several buttons which can be used for the rapid execution of various commands:

- The Navigator button to move to named ranges
- The @ function button
- The Cancel button to discontinue input
- The Confirm button to confirm input in the currently active cell.

The area to the right of this is the Contents box. This displays the contents of the currently active cell.

d) The SmartIcons

The so-called SmartIcons are located under the Edit line. This is also referred to as the Toolbar. This is a set of frequently-used commands which are presented as icons. They can be activated directly by clicking instead of in a roundabout way via the menus.

In this way, you are able to, for instance, save or print a file quickly and easily, by clicking on the relevant icon. There are four sets of icons. The set shown depends on the selection in the worksheet. You may select a different set yourself. The first set of icons have the following significance, from left to right:

Icon	Application
Open existing file	Opens an existing file
Save current file	Saves current file
Print current selection	Prints a selected range
Print preview	Shows an example of the printed range
Undo previous command	Revokes previous command
Cut data to the Clipboard	Remove selected range and transfer it to the Clipboard
Copy to the Clipboard	Copies a selected range to the Clipboard
Paste from the Clipboard	Extract a selected range from the Clipboard and include it in the worksheet
Add figures above or left	Adds up the data in the selected range
B, I, U	Specifies the font attributes: bold, italics, underlined
Three alignment icons	Align the cell contents, respectively left, centred and right
Enter a series in a selected range	Enter a consecutive seies of data in a range

Select various objects	Draws a frame around various objects to be selected
Four graphic icons	Draw an arrow, rectangle, oval or text block
Make a macro button	Assigns a button to a macro
Create a diagram	Create a diagram of a selected range of data
Next set of SmartIcons	Selects the next icon set.

There is also the interesting facility of being able to create a set of icons entirely geared to your own requirements. As soon as you know what these requirements are going to be, once you have become familiar with the program, you can begin compiling this set. To do this, select the *SmartIcons* option from the *Tools* menu.

Note: It is not possible to use the SmartIcons if you do not have a mouse. This is the only way to activate the icons.

e) Worksheet tab

This line can be used when working with several worksheets. It allows you to switch quickly to another worksheet or to insert a new worksheet behind the current one. A tab appears for each worksheet. You can switch to the required worksheet by clicking once on the tab. You can also alter the name of the worksheet by means double clicking on this tab.

f) Worksheet area

This is the area in the middle of the screen containing the cells. Data are entered and processed in these cells. It is possible to open several windows simultaneously on the screen.

g) Scroll bars

If you are working with a mouse, the scroll bars at the
bottom and at the right-hand side of the screen are particularly important. They indicate the horizontal and vertical position of the current insertion point in relation to
the entire worksheet. In addition, you can browse
through the various parts of the worksheet by clicking
on the scroll bars:

■ The vertical scroll bar at the right-hand side of the
window enables you to browse through the worksheet from top to bottom.
■ The horizontal scroll bar at the bottom of the window
enables you to move to the left or right of the section
of the worksheet currently being shown.

There is also another scroll block between the scroll arrows which indicates the approximate position of the
window in relation to the entire worksheet. You can drag
this block using the mouse to any chosen position in
order to display another part of the worksheet on the
screen. This is a quick method of moving from the beginning to the end of the worksheet.

1.5   Basic aspects of the program

The 1-2-3/W program is, in principle, a menu-driven
program. Thus, if you wish to execute a certain command, such as printing or saving a worksheet, you must
select the corresponding command from a menu. We
shall discuss this topic in more depth in the next chapter.

An alternative method of implementing a command is to
press specified function keys. A list of the most important keys is displayed in the appendix.

1.5.1 Implementing commands

By giving certain commands, you activate the computer
into carrying out certain options. The 1-2-3/W program
contains a great many commands, but it is possible to
execute fundamental procedures using only a limited
number of these.

When giving commands, proceed as follows:

■ First activate one of the *menu names* on the menu
bar. The activated menu opens displaying a list of options.
■ Select the required command from the menu.
■ A *dialog box* may subsequently appear in which you
must enter further specifications. Enter these specifications at the appropriate positions.

Note: The names of the commands in the menus may
alter if you have defined a range in the worksheet as a
Query Table or if you have selected a chart.

Activating the menus

There are three ways of opening a menu on the menu
bar:

■ Place the mouse pointer on the menu name and click
on the left-hand mouse button.
■ Press the Alt key, hold it down and press the underlined letter in the required menu name.
■ Press the F10 function key, select the required menu
by pressing the Cursor Right key and then press
Enter.

Note: It is, of course, possible to cancel a command.
Click outside the menu or press Esc twice.

Exercise 1-1:
Activate the *File* menu by means of the three methods described above. The screen will look something like this:

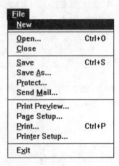

The File menu

Keep in mind that it is not always possible to execute all options. If an option is not available, it is displayed in grey in the menu list. Open the *Edit* menu in order to see what is meant here.

Selecting commands

When you have opened a menu, there are again various ways of selecting commands:

■ Move the cursor to the required option and press Enter.
■ Press the underlined letter in the command. If you wish to print a worksheet for instance, press the letter P once you have opened the *File* menu.
■ Place the mouse pointer on the required command and click on the left mouse button.

Some commands are executed immediately after being activated. However, 1-2-3/W often requires additional information. A dialog window will appear if this is the case.

When selecting and activating commands, pay attention to the following aspects:

■ If three dots are shown behind the command, a dialog box will appear first.
■ If an arrow is shown behind a command, a submenu containing additional option will appear when the command is activated.
■ Confirmation will be required in a number of cases. For example, if you attempt to terminate the program without having previously saved the modifications to the worksheet, you will be asked to confirm your intention.
■ If you wish to discontinue the execution of a command, you can close the activated menu by positioning the mouse pointer outside the menu and clicking on the left mouse button. You can also press the Esc key.

1.5.2   Further command specification

Commands in the menu which have three dots are not implemented immediately. The program first requires additional information.

Filling in the dialog box

A dialog window is displayed enabling you to enter additional data for the command. Various options are shown. These options are divided into the following categories:

■ **Text box:** You can enter extra information in a text box without restriction. This information may consist of text or numbers. For instance: a file name. You can also adopt the program proposals where appropriate.

■ **Options list:** You can make a choice from the list of options shown. The currently active item in the list is highlighted. In the case of lengthy lists, not all items

can be shown. Use the scroll bars to move up and
down through the list.

■ **Pull-down menus:** These lists can be recognized by
the arrow at the right of a small window displaying
only one item. If you wish to examine the contents of
this list, click on the arrow or activate the list using the
Alt key in combination with the underlined letter and
then press Cursor Down.

■ **Check box:** A check box is a square box enabling
you to select an option which can be chosen independent of other options. By placing a cross in the
box, the option is activated. In certain cases, this box
will be shown in grey. This means that the selected
range has various settings for this option.

■ **Options button:** Option buttons are always grouped
together in a frame. Only one option can be chosen
from this group. A small circle is shown in front of the
option. When the option is activated, the circle contains a black spot.

Exercise 1-2:

Several of the options outlined above can be examined
by selecting the *Page Setup* option from the *File* menu.
The following options then appear in the subsequent
dialog box:

■ Text boxes: Margins (Top, Bottom, Left, Right),
Header, Footer, Columns, Rows, Size.
■ The Show group contains three check boxes: Work-
sheet frame, Grid lines and Drawn objects.
■ The Orientation group contains two option buttons:
Portrait and Landscape.

In addition, there are the so-called command buttons in
the dialog window. These activate or cancel the command. The selected command button has a dark border. If you press Enter, the relevant action is carried out.

The text on the button indicates what is going to take place.

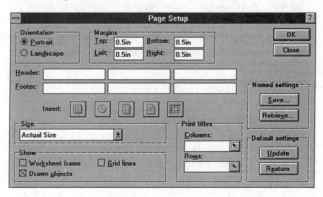

Page Setup dialog window

An example of pull-down menus can be gained by selecting the *Open* option from the *File* menu. The following dialog window appears:

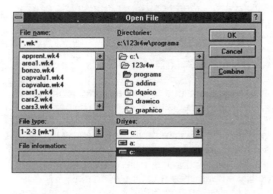

Examples of pull-down menus

Note: It may also be the case that certain options in dialog windows are not available due to the influence of settings elswhere. They are then shown in grey.

Prior to a command actually being implemented, the computer must receive a clear command to perform the action. This occurs by clicking on the OK button or pressing Enter (if this button is active) in the dialog window. When the command has been executed, the program normally returns to the worksheet area. However, the computer can also react to the execution of a command in two other ways:

■ With an error message. If, for instance, you select the *Print* option from the *File* menu while the printer is not connected, the computer will respond to the OK instruction with the error message: 'The printer on LPT1 is out of paper or is not connected to your computer...'

■ With a request for additional information. A typical example of this may occur at the termination of a file or the program itself. In order to prevent unintentional loss, 1-2-3/W asks whether you wish to save the modifications made. By pressing Y(es) you can confirm your intention to do so. N(o) means you do not wish to save the alterations made. Press Esc or activate Cancel in order to cancel the command.

1.6   Working with SmartIcons

Commands and functions which are frequently used can be implemented quickly and easily using the so-called *SmartIcons*, located under the Edit line. The required command or function can be executed by clicking on the appropriate icon.

The procedure is as follows:

■ Place the pointer on the icon representing the command or function you wish to execute.
■ Press the left mouse button in order to carry out the command or macro.

Try this out by clicking on the first first icon on the line.
The *Open File* dialog box appears on the screen.

You can also move the icon set to a different position on
the screen if you wish. The options provided by the icon
set can also be changed. To do this, select the *Smart-
Icons* option from the *Tools* menu. The following dialog
window appears:

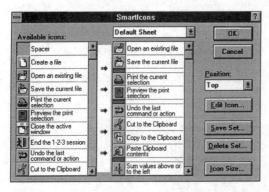

SmartIcons dialog window

Altering the position of SmartIcons

SmartIcons can be placed at one of four fixed positions
on the screen: Top, Right, Bottom, Left. In addition,
there is also the Floating option which enables you to
place the SmartIcon set at any chosen position on the
screen. To do this, select *Tools, SmartIcons*. Select
Floating from the Position box and click on OK. You can
then drag the icon set to any required position by clicking on the icon box, holding the button down and dragging the frame to the new position.

Try out all the variants by activating an option and clicking on OK. The icon set appears at the new position.

Hiding the SmartIcons

If you do not wish to use the SmartIcons, or wish to create more room on the screen, you can hide the Smart-
Icons. To do this, click on the icon symbol (the three
small squares) on the status line at the bottom of the
screen. A list of options appears. Click on *Hide Smart-
Icons*. Try this out, and then restore them by clicking on
the symbol once more and choosing *Show SmartIcons*.

Altering the appearance of the icons

If you wish to alter the appearance of the icons, select
Tools, SmartIcons. Then select *Edit Icon*. The following
dialog box appears:

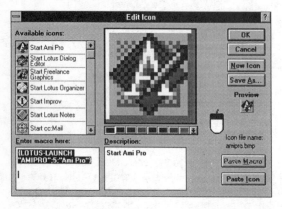

Edit SmartIcon dialog window

1.7   Working with the mouse

Many tasks in 1-2-3/W can be executed much more
quickly using the mouse than using the keyboard, such
as activating commands, working in dialog windows, or
when applying special functions like marking ranges,
determining column width and altering window sizes.

The shape of the pointer determines the type of action which you can carry out at that moment. A list is given below of the most common options:

pointer type	screen position	actions
arrow	menu bar, worksheet, scroll bars, status bar	select commands, move cell pointer, activate a window, select options in dialog boxes.
white two-headed arrow	window frame, window corner	change size of the windows in horizontal and vertical directions.
black two-headed arrow	row and column edges	alter column width and row height.
insert symbol	edit line	enter and alter data.
hour glass	anywhere	wait until process is complete.
hand with pointing finger	help index	provides help in the help window.
hand	cell or chart	moving the object to a new position.
pencil	chart	make a drawing in a chart.

Example: Place the pointer on a window frame. The arrow changes into a two-headed arrow enabling you to alter the size of the window using the mouse.

When describing the various mouse manoeuvres, certain terminology is applied (see overleaf).

manoeuvre	effect
Point	Move the pointer to a certain screen element (icon or command) in order to carry out an action; the mouse must be moved over a flat surface (preferably a mouse mat).
Click	Press and release the mouse button; the left mouse button is most frequently used.
Double click	Press the mouse button twice in rapid succession.
Drag	Press and hold down left mouse button and move pointer over the screen.
Release	Conclude the execution of a command or marking.

1.8   1-2-3/W Help

1-2-3/W has a Help function which can be activated if you are no longer sure just what to do to implement a command. This function is especially convenient when learning how to use the program.

There are three ways of activating Help:

■ a general summons to look for something in the index
■ a context-oriented summons
■ a thematic Help instruction.

In all cases, the Help function is closed by selecting the *Exit* option from the *File* menu in Help.

The general Help summons

If you require general Help information, click on the *Help* menu in the menu bar, or press Alt-H. The Help menu appears.

Help menu

The menu options are as follows:

command	significance
Contents	Displays a list of all Help categories.
Search	Displays a dialog box in which you can specify a topic about which you wish to know more.
Using Help	Provides information about the use of 1-2-3/W Help.
Keyboard	Provides a summary of keyboard functions, including shortcut keys and other special keys.
How Do I?	Provides a summary of common tasks in 1-2-3/W.
For Upgraders	Provides information about new and advanced 1-2-3/W applications.
Tutorial	Starts up the 1-2-3/W tutorial.
About 1-2-3...	Displays information about the version number and the copyright.

If you select the *Contents* option, a window appears containing a list of topics. You can select one of these topics in one of the following ways:

- Place the pointer on the required topic. As soon as the pointer turns into a hand, click on the left mouse button.
- Press the Tab key to move the cursor to the required topic. Then press Enter.

Select the topic *Mouse* using one of the methods described above. The following window appears on the
screen:

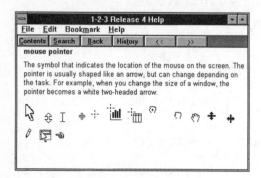

Mouse Help window

Place the pointer on the scroll block in the vertical scroll
bar. Hold down the left mouse button and drag the block
downwards. While you are dragging, the block will remain visible at the top of the screen, but the shadow of
the block moves with the pointer. When you release the
button, the window displays the corresponding text segment.

Context-oriented Help

It may occur that you are no longer completely sure of
the next step when you are carrying out a particular
command, for instance when using the *Find & Replace*
function from the *Edit* menu. You can summon context-
oriented help at such moments. Select the option and
press F1, the Help key. The Help window appears displaying information about the currently active function.
The Help window contains information about the
chosen topic.

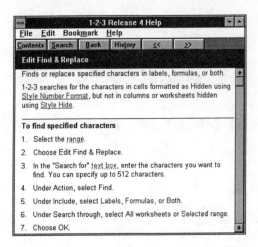

Help window for Edit, Find & Replace

When you have read the information and wish to return
to the worksheet or dialog window, close the Help window by selecting the *Exit* option from the *File* menu in
the Help window.

In principle, it is possible to summon a context-oriented
Help window for each command or dialog window. This
occurs as follows:

current situation	effect of F1
Cursor in the text	The Help index appears
Selected menu	Context-oriented Help about the
Command	command
Activated dialog	Context-oriented Help about the
window	dialog window

The Help texts displayed can also be printed out on the
printer. To do this, open the *File* menu in the Help window and select *Print Topic*.

1.9 Information for converts from DOS

In order to facilitate the switch from the DOS version to Windows, it is also possible to activate the classic Lotus 1-2-3 menu using the slash (/) in the 1-2-3/W version. The menu appears in a separate window.

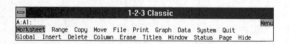

The Lotus 1-2-3 Classic menu

You can gain more information about this menu from the Prisma book _Lotus 1-2-3 2.4_ which has also been published in this series.

1.10 Quitting the program

The program can be terminated by selecting _Exit_ from the _File_ menu. It is advisable to save the file you have just been working on if you wish to process the data further at a later date. If you have not already done this, a dialog window appears in which you will be given the chance of saving the file. Then the program is terminated and you will return to the program from which you started 1-2-3/W, probably the Windows Program Manager.

Summary of chapter 1

■ 1-2-3/W is an integrated program for the personal computer which contains three function areas: spreadsheets, charts and database.
■ There are two methods of starting the 1-2-3/W program: by clicking on the Lotus 1-2-3 Release 4 icon in the Program Manager, or by double-clicking on the 123W.EXE file in the File Manager.
■ Commands in 1-2-3/W are mostly menu-driven. Function keys are also available for certain options.

Use of the mouse makes the program much more straightforward.

■ Diverse options are presented in the dialog windows: text boxes, check boxes, option buttons and pull-down menus.

■ The SmartIcons, which are normally located under the Edit line, enable you to execute frequently-used commands and functions quickly and easily. The composition and position of the SmartIcon set can be altered.

■ The program provides an integrated Help program. If necessary, context-oriented help can be summoned to clarify topics and commands.

2   Spreadsheets

2.1   Basic concepts and application possibilities

Information which is processed in the office and in management in general, can frequently be presented in the form of tables. Making and editing tables using traditional methods is often rather laborious. This mostly involves considerable calculation and any subsequent alteration leads to time-consuming recalculation.

Spreadsheet programs have been developed to deal with this kind of problem. In these, an electronic form is created on the screen. The user is provided with a number of cells, a combination of rows and columns. These cells can be freely used. This electronic form is called a *spreadsheet* or *worksheet*.

In this worksheet, each cell consists of an empty space which can be filled in using text or numbers in the chosen application area. Formulas can also be entered, allowing relations between cells to be constructed. This provides the possibility of calculating several alternatives quickly and smoothly in the light of various data.

The illustration on the following page shows a summary of the basic structure of a simple spreadsheet.

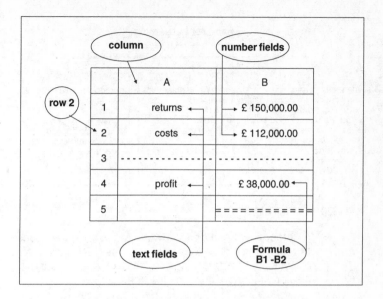

Diagram of an electronic worksheet

1-2-3/W is able to construct *three-dimensional spreadsheets*. This means that several worksheets which refer to the same area but which deal with different elements in that area are combined within a single file.

The application area of spreadsheet programs is extremely large. The main objective is the support of procedures which involve planning and management. Although applications dealing with company business management are clearly in the majority, there are also substantial possibilities within the technical and scientific fields and also, quite simply, in personal situations. The following summary shows examples of familiar applications within the three areas mentioned.

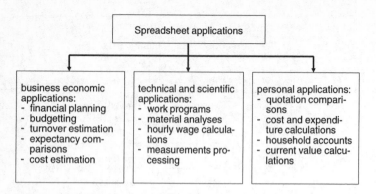

Summary of application areas

A spreadsheet can bring advantages even in the case of relatively small tables and, of course, the facility of operation and time-saving are greater the larger the tables and the more complex the formulas.

The most important benefits of a PC spreadsheet are:

Time-consuming and tedious calculation becomes unnecessary. This arises from the fact that the program can be used as a calculator. In addition, a large number of convenient functions are available, such as the determination of the sum or the calculation of the average value of a series of numbers, for which it is not necessary to introduce a difficult and lengthy formula.

Quick corrections (entering, deleting, replacing). Later alterations to the form or contents, or correction of errors, are no exception when making monetary calculations. In cases like these, the computer program adjusts the form and the contents to the newly entered data. Often an immediate test is carried out with regard to logical precision.

When number values are corrected, a recalculation of all relevant values takes place. Working with formulas makes a direct and rapid adjustment possible without extensive alterations to the spreadsheet.

Several versions of a problem solution can be worked out, for instance, various market or personnel situations.

Hypothetical questions can be easily solved. For example, using the returns figures per article, the change in the break-even point if the selling price of an article rises by a certain amount.

2.2 The structure of the worksheet

The 1-2-3/W program is able to create three-dimensional files. These may contain up to 256 worksheets, each containing a maximum of 8192 rows and 256 columns. The points of intersection of the rows and columns are the *cells*. Thus, a table consists of a maximum of 2,097,152 cells (or fields) which can hold text, numbers or formulas.

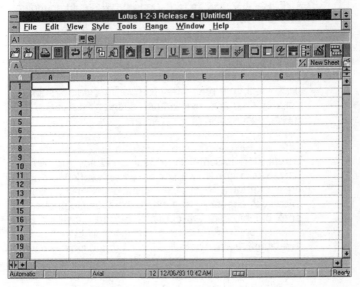

Worksheet window

When 1-2-3/W has been started up, the screen will display a worksheet (it is advisable to display the worksheet at maximum size).

The opening window was already shown in chapter 1.
The actual worksheet area which occupies the majority
of the screen is examined more closely here. This area
normally occupies 20 rows and 8 columns which have a
width of 9 characters. This means that 160 cells are displayed in each window.

The cells contain no data as yet. The assignment of
contents to the cells occurs by entering data or by calculation of formulas. In both cases, it is necessary to
determine the exact position of the cell by specifying the
appropriate column and row.

Each *column* is identified by one or two letters, the first
twenty six with the letters A - Z, those following with AA
- ZZ, BA - BZ and so forth up to IV. The column indication is shown along the top of the worksheet.

Rows, on the other hand, are identified by numbers,
from 1 to 8192. The row numbers are located at the left-
hand side of the worksheet. In order to address a particular cell, it is necessary to specify a combination of
column letter and row number, such as A13 or B2. A13
refers to the cell in column A, row 13.

One of the cells has a dark frame. This is the *cell
pointer*. This indicates the current work position and can
be moved to another position on the worksheet using
the cursor keys or certain function keys. The positioning
of the cell pointer determines the cell to which the next
entry or instruction will apply.

The summary on the following page indicates how the
cell pointer can be moved using the cursor or function
keys.

position	key(s)
per column	cursor left/right
per row	cursor up/down
screen left-/rightwards	Ctrl-cursor left/right
screen up/downwards	PgUp/PgDn
top left in spreadsheet	Home
jump to the limit in cursor direction	End, cursor key

Moving the cell pointer using the mouse is equally easy. Just click on the cell in which you wish to make an entry. If the required cell is not shown on the screen, use the scroll bars to move to the appropriate part of the worksheet.

You can also address the required cell directly by means of F5, the GoTo key. You achieve the same effect by using the *Go To* option in the *Edit* menu.

As mentioned, 1-2-3/W is able to compile several worksheets in three-dimensional form and to save them. It is possible to link a total of 256 worksheets in this way. Each worksheet is indicated by its own letter so that it is always clear which worksheet is meant. When several worksheets are being dealt with, the cell address indication is always preceded by the relevant worksheet letter and a colon. The complete address of a cell will then be as follows for example: B:E14. This refers to the cell in column E, row 14 of worksheet B.

As the cell pointer moves, the cell address changes. This is shown in the upper part of the screen, for example C6.

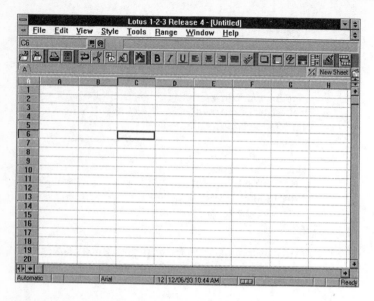

Changing the position of the cell pointer

The Control Panel

The so-called Control Panel is located above the work area. It consists of the following elements:

■ the title bar
■ the menu bar
■ the edit line, containing the selection indicator, the navigator, the function selector, the Cancel and Confirm buttons (only shown when input is made) and the contents box.
■ the SmartIcons
■ the worksheet tabs

The status bar

The date and time are shown on the status line at the bottom of the screen. Here you can also select the font you wish to use and the size of the letter (the so-called *point size*). You can also select a different SmartIcon set. Information about the current status is also shown here. The status indicator has the following possibilities:

status	significance
Calc	Recalculation is being performed by means of the F9 key.
Circ	A formula with a circular reference.
Cmd	1-2-3/W is running a macro.
End	End has been pressed in combination with a cursor key.
Group	The current file is in group mode.
Pr	Cell protection is activated.
Step	Running a macro in STEP mode.
Zoom	Full-screen display of the current worksheet.

The most common variants of the mode indicator are displayed in the list below.

mode	significance
Edit	When altering cell contents, after pressing F2.
Label	When entering text.
Menu	When the menu bar is active and commands are being given.
Point	When specifying a range.
Ready	Ready to accept input.
Value	When entering a number or a formula.
Wait	When a command is being implemented.

2.3   Preparing a table

That there are many applications for the spreadsheet
has already been mentioned. However, before you
begin to solve a practical problem using the computer, it
is useful to thoroughly analyse the nature of the problem. Only then will you be sure that a spreadsheet will
be created which provides the desired solution. The
greater the consideration, the smaller the chance of errors.

In order to make a efficient calculation model, the following questions should be answered:

■ Which kind of results should the computer come up
  with?
■ Which information is needed to solve the problem?
■ Which calculations need to be carried out to produce
  the desired results?

2.4   Altering the default settings

General planning may make it useful to change some
default settings. 1-2-3/W has default settings for:

■ the font used
■ the width of the individual columns
■ the way in which texts are aligned
■ the way in which numbers are displayed
■ the colour display in the cells.

These default settings can be altered using the *Worksheet Defaults* option from the *Style* menu. Activate this
option.

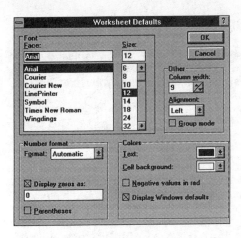

The Worksheet Defaults window

This window displays detailed information about the global parameters which have been set and the hardware options. The default column width, for instance, is nine characters and text is normally left-aligned. The list below describes the various options:

options	significance
Font	Face, Size: Specify the letter type and size.
Column width	The default setting for the column width in the worksheets.
Alignment	The standard form of alignment.
Group mode	Check box to switch group mode on or off.
Number format	The method of expression of numbers.
Display zeros as	Determine the display of zero values.
Colors	Specify the colours to be used for text, cell background and negative values. The Windows standard settings are normally applied.

2.4.1   Changing the default column width

As already mentioned, 1-2-3/W has a default column width of nine characters. You can change this if you wish by adjusting the settings in the *Worksheet Defaults* dialog window.

Exercise 2-1:

Set the column width to twelve characters.

When you have entered the new value and have confirmed the command, the program returns to the worksheet. Now there are only six columns visible on the screen (A to F instead of A to H). The figure below illustrates this:

Column width 12 has now become the standard setting for all columns in the worksheet. Nevertheless, it is still possible to give individual columns a different width. To do this, make use of the *Column Width* option in the *Style* menu; this suspends the default column width setting for the specified columns. Columns may be assigned a width ranging from 1 to 240 characters.

The row height can be altered in much the same way. You can change the default setting of 14 points in the *Row Height* dialog box by selecting this option from the *Style* menu.

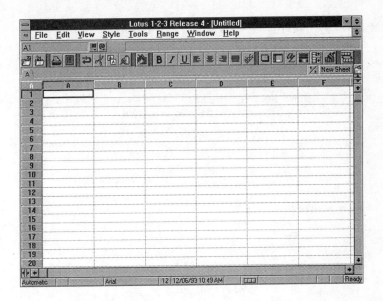

The screen layout has changed

2.4.2 Altering the default alignment

The alignment of text also has a standard setting. In general, texts (labels) are left-aligned throughout the whole worksheet. Changes to this can be made by selecting the *Worksheet Defaults* option from the *Style* menu. The alterations are made by opening the Alignment pull-down menu in the dialog box. You can choose either Left, Right or Center.

Note: It is also possible to select another form of alignment by placing a certain character in a cell: for instance, the apostrophe (') produces left-alignment, the caret symbol (^) centres, and inverted commas produces right-alignment. Alteration to the default settings does not influence cells which have already been aligned.

2.4.3   Altering the default number format

In 1-2-3/W, numbers are normally displayed as real
numbers. This applies both to numbers which are entered and to results which are calculated. In this, the
values are registered to a precision of fifteen decimal
points regardless of the format used.

The default setting of numeric values can be altered
using the *Worksheet Defaults* option from the *Style*
menu. Click on the arrows in the Format group of the
Number format window to see all the options:

Format group from Number Format dialog window

Fixed	for display of a fixed number of decimals
Scientific	for display in exponential form
Currency	for display of numbers with a particular unit of currency
, Comma	for separation of thousands
General	standard display in real numbers
+/-	for display as bar chart
Percent	to add the percentage symbol
Text	to display formulas on the screen
Hidden	to suppress display of information on the screen.
Automatic	the initial default number format is Auto-matic. 1-2-3/W formats data correspond-ing to the way they are entered. See *Help, Number Format*.
Label	for the display of formulas on the screen.
Date/time	to choose a certain notation for date and time (five date and four time methods of notation are possible).

Finally, pay attention to the following remarks:

■ Global changes do not have any effect on the format of cells which has been determined using the *Number Format* option from the *Style* menu. This command will also be dealt with and further explained in subsequent chapters of this book.

■ The format commands only influence the display of the data. The data themselves remain unchanged. For instance, calculations involving decimal numbers are carried out, even if the results are only to be shown as whole numbers. If you wish to use whole numbers in the calculation, you must specify this clearly (using the @ROUND function).

When cells contain zeros, either as data or as the result of calculations, you can specify how these are to be displayed. This is done in the *Worksheet Defaults* dialog window which is opened by selecting this option from the *Style* menu. Select the appropriate text box and type the text or character which is to represent the number 0. Normally, you would accept the default setting '0', or you might wish to specify the label 'zero' or even an empty cell.

2.4.4   Working with the GROUP mode

The characteristic feature of three-dimensional spreadsheets is the possibility of managing different worksheets in one common file. If these worksheets are constructed in the same way (for instance with the same column width, format and alignment), it is possible to alter all these settings simultaneously. To do this, the GROUP mode must be activated.

Switching the Group mode on and off takes place in the *Worksheet Defaults* window (from the *Style* menu) by means of the corresponding check box. When this option is activated, the settings which apply to the current worksheet are automatically assigned to all other worksheets in the file. The cell pointer is then located on the

same cell in all worksheets. Actions such as cutting,
pasting and formatting are executed in all worksheets
simultaneously. When dealing with this topic, pay close
attention to the following:

■ The status bar at the bottom of the screen will indicate whether the Group Mode is switched on or not.
■ When the Group mode is switched off again, the settings which were brought into force when the mode
was switched on are not automatically adjusted back
to the original situation.
■ If the Group mode is switched off, each worksheet is
regarded as being a separate entity.
■ An extensive example of working with the Group
mode is given in chapter 7: *Three-dimensional worksheets.*

2.4.5   Setting default values for the program start

Additional alterations to the default settings can be
made using the *User Setup* option from the *Tools* menu.
The following dialog window appears:

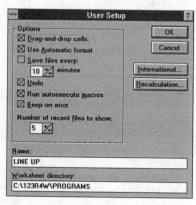

User Setup dialog box

You can specify several general settings for worksheets including the currency symbol and the date and time format (via International) and the method of recalculation for worksheets.

1-2-3/W provides the facility of specifying certain settings which will be active from the startup of the program. Among other things, these deal with:

- the directory for retrieving files (Worksheet directory)
- various international and date and time settings (International).

The settings which you specify here are stored in a separate configuration file. This enables them to be activated immediately when the program is started up. The options in the User Setup window have the following significance:

option	significance
Drag-and-drop cells	Ensures that cells can be dragged and copied by dragging them with the mouse.
Use Automatic format	If you remove the cross here, General will become the default format.
Save files every:	Specify here the interval between automatic backup; this is normally 10 minutes.
Undo	Switches the Undo function on/off (*Edit* menu, *Undo* option).
Run autoexecute macros	Determines whether an autoexecute macro (AUTOEXEC) should be run immediately at the program start.
Beep on error	Switches an acoustic signal on/off in case of error.
Worksheet directory	Determines the drive and directory for saving and retrieving files.

The International button opens a dialog box containing options to specify the separator, the currency symbol and date and time settings. The dialog box appears as follows:

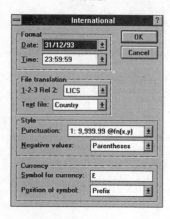

The International dialog box

2.4.6 Determining the calculation method

The order of sequence of calculation is standard in as much as the value of a formula is calculated only when all the values needed to make the calculation are known. This default setting can be changed by means of the _User Setup_ option from the _Tools_ menu. Activate the Recalculation box. The following window appears:

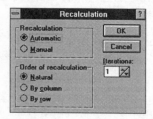

The Recalculation dialog box

This dialog box can be used to precisely determine when and in which order of sequence the formulas in the worksheet are to be recalculated.

In addition to the Natural order of recalculation, there are two other options:

■ **By column**: the values in column A are calculated first, then those in column B etc.
■ **By row**: the values in row 1 are calculated first, then those in row 2 etc.

The default setting, Natural, is normally the most useful method of recalculation. It is really only worthwhile specifying one of the other options when direct checks have to be executed.

With reference to the actual moment of recalculation, there are two alternatives:

■ **Automatic**: when the contents of a cell have been altered, the worksheet is immediately recalculated.
■ **Manual**: when the contents of a cell have been altered, the table is recalculated only after the CALC key (F9) has been pressed. This allows the specification of new data in large worksheets to take place more quickly and easily.

Finally, the Iteration option enables repeated calculation. Specify the number of repetitions required.

Summary of chapter 2

■ A spreadsheet provides the user with an electronic form consisting of columns and rows. In the case of three-dimensional spreadsheets, it is possible to combine different worksheets.
■ Texts, numbers and formulas can be entered in the cells.
■ A spreadsheet can be used for commercial, technical and private applications. This enables many calcula-

tion, writing, presentation and file management tasks to be carried out simply and straightforwardly.

■ Spreadsheets provide important benefits of time-saving in extensive calculations, easy editing and correction at a later date, and a convenient way of working out alternatives.

■ 1-2-3/W provides a worksheet with 8192 rows and 256 columns. The cell, the work position in the worksheet, is, in fact, the intersection of the row and the column.

■ Columns are indicated by letters, rows by numbers.

■ Addressing a cell occurs by specifying the column letter and row number.

■ The 1-2-3/W window consists of two main areas: the Control Panel at the top of the screen and the work area which normally contains 160 cells.

■ Before deciding to assign a problem to the computer, you should first consider the structure and the format of the worksheet.

■ The default settings for column width, number format and alignment can be altered using the *Worksheet Defaults* option from the *Style* menu.

3 Compiling a simple worksheet

When all settings have been defined, the input of data can begin. This takes place using the keyboard. A clear distinction must be made between the following forms:

- input of text, called 'labels' in 1-2-3/W
- input of numbers
- input of formulas for calculation.

It is advisable to enter the texts and the independent number values first and then the formulas which make it possible to link cells. ·

In order to learn the basic functions of the 1-2-3/W spreadsheet, we shall get down to work by constructing a simple two-dimensional worksheet in the exercise 'Turnover calculation'.

Exercise 3-1: Calculation of turnover

Create a 1-2-3/W worksheet to solve the following problem:

Based on the estimated monthly turnover, the expected annual turnover and the maximum and minimum monthly turnover are to be calculated. The result should be displayed in the form shown overleaf.

Month	Turnover x £1000
january	150
february	212
march	222
april	318
may	344
june	551
july	180
august	166
september	300
october	345
november	433
december	335
total	3556
maximum	551
minimum	150

3.1   Entering text

A fundamental rule when making any entry at all is that you first have to go to the cell where the input is to be made. In the example shown, we should select A2 as the first active cell.

When text is being entered, it appears in both the Contents box and the currently active cell. At the same time, the mode block in the lower right-hand corner changes from READY to LABEL. For this reason, text input is often referred to as label input. To confirm the text entry, you have to press Enter. The mode changes again from LABEL to READY.

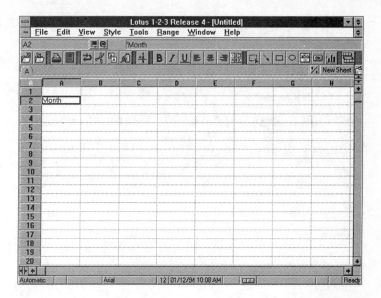

Entering text in a worksheet

The text being entered also appears on the edit line. The apostrophe in front of the text indicates that you are dealing with a text line.

As well as using the Enter key, text can also be moved to the cell by means of one of the cursor keys. This can be useful if a series of texts has to be entered, since the following cell is immediately activated for the registration of new text. If you press a cursor key, the cell pointer is moved in the direction of the cursor key and the next input can take place.

The general procedure for the input of a series of texts is as follows:

■ Place the cell pointer at the first input cell using a cursor key or by clicking on it.
■ Enter the text, for instance 'january'.
■ Confirm the input and activate the next cell using the relevant cursor key.

■ Enter the next text, for instance 'february'.
■ Confirm the input as above.

Normally, the texts which have been entered are left-aligned in the current cell of the table. This is clear in the figure below:

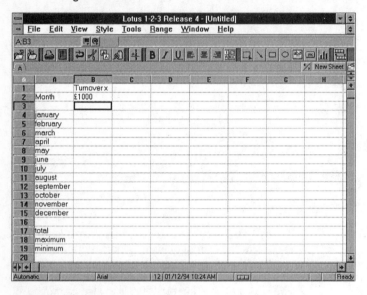

Worksheet with all text data

In addition, you will observe that if information has already been entered in a cell, it will be removed if new information is entered there. The previous information is then irretrievably lost.

Texts which are too lengthy to fit the column width extend into the next cell if no data are entered there. If this cell does contain data, only the text which fits into the first cell will be shown. (It may seem as if the data in the second cell is removed, but it appears once more when you press Enter or a cursor key to confirm the input.)

Nevertheless, it will undoubtedly occur that when entering information you will place it in the wrong cell or you may forget a character. In cases like these, the following correction possibilities are available:

■ If an error is seen directly at the input, it can be corrected using the Backspace key.

■ Using Esc, a text which has been typed but not yet confirmed can be cancelled.

■ If you have accidentally placed information in a cell where no information should be located, you can undo this by activating the cell again and pressing the Del key. You can also do this by selecting the *Clear* option from the *Edit* menu.

■ In principle, there are two possibilities to correct erroneous input in a cell. The correct input can simply be written over the old information by activating the cell once more and entering the information again. In addition, it is also possible to edit the text. This is especially applicable to larger amounts of data which have already been entered. To do this, the cell in question has to be activated by double-clicking on it. Then modifications can be made to the contents. It is also possible to activate the EDIT mode by pressing the F2 function key. It is now possible to move through the text using the cursor keys and to make corrections at the required positions, using the Del key if necessary. Confirm the modifications using Enter or by moving to another cell using the cursor keys. You can also click on the Confirm button on the Edit line.

3.2   Entering numbers

When the text data have been entered, you can continue with the number values which are already known. Activate the cell in which the input should be placed, B4 for instance. In the case of a number (in this case 150), the program registers that immediately. The mode indicator changes immediately from Ready to Value. When confirmed the mode changes to Ready once more.

The general procedure when entering values is as follows:

- Activate the cell which is to receive information by clicking on it or by moving to it using the cursor keys.
- Enter the value, for instance 150.
- Confirm the imput using Enter or one of the cursor keys or click on the Confirm button.

The Enter key is normally used if you do not have to enter any more numbers. If numbers have to be entered consecutively, it is better to make use of the cursor keys to directly activate the next cell. Now enter all the numbers from the example. Correction of numbers input takes place in the same way as with text input. When all information has been entered, the table should appear as in the table below:

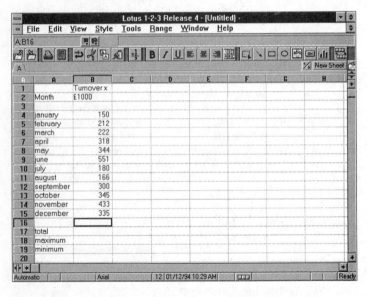

The worksheet containing the data

There is one thing which is immediately obvious - in contrast to the text, the numbers are right-aligned.

Note:

■ In 1-2-3/W, information can be entered in various formats. For example, a number can be entered as a percentage (e.g. 50%) or as an exponential value (5.23E+0.3). We shall return to the topic of notation later.

■ A number must begin with a cypher or with one of the following characters: . + - $ (

■ A number can consist of a maximum of 512 characters.

■ Spaces are not valid when entering thousands. In addition only one decimal point may be specified in a number.

■ If the number entered is broader than the column, a series of asterisks is shown in this cell. However, this does not influence the number stored in memory. If the column is widened, the number is displayed in full.

■ The decimal separator is the point.

3.3 Entering formulas

Using formulas, a relation can be created between two or more cells in a table. This means that results can be calculated automatically. In addition, it is possible to quickly work out the variants relevant to a certain problem.

The general components of a formula are:

■ independent values, for example 14, -5
■ cell addresses, for example A13
■ certain calculation signs, the so-called *operators*.

In complex applications, a formula may also consist of strings (texts, like names), range specifications and functions (the so-called @-functions).

3.3.1   Formula structure

In the case of formula input, it is necessary to first activate the cell in which the required result is to be placed.
Subsequently, you should specify, by entering a plus
sign (+), that a formula is about to be entered. Then the
formula may be entered.

Procedure for formulas in 1-2-3/W:

■ No spaces may occur in formulas.
■ A formula may consist of a maximum of 512 characters.
■ A plus sign must precede a formula if a cell address
  is specified instead of a number.
■ Knowledge of the calculation signs is essential for the
  formal structure of the formula.

The calculation signs, which activate the execution of
certain operations, are also called *operators*. The important operators in 1-2-3/W are listed below:

operator	significance	order of preference
^	power	1 (highest)
+	positive value	2
-	negative value	2
*	multiply	3
/	divide	3
+	add	4
-	subtract	4
=	equals	5
<	smaller than	5
<=	smaller than or equal to	5
>	greater than	5
>=	greater than or equal to	5
<>	not equal to	5
#NOT#	logical negative	6
#AND#	logical AND relation	7
#OR#	logical OR relation	7
&	string link	7 (lowest)

In the summary, in addition to the significance of the various operators, a hierarchical rank number has been allocated. This indicates the order in which 1-2-3/W executes the calculations if several operators are included in the formula. The rules applying to this are:

■ Operations with a low rank number are implemented first.
■ In the case of operations with the same rank number, the calculation takes place from left to right.
■ If brackets are included, the operations between the brackets are executed first. Within the brackets the rank numbers remain valid.

Examine the following formula. The order of execution is shown underneath:

```
A13-A5((A7+20)*0.13)/450
   4        1   2       3
```

In the example dealing with the calculation of turnover, formulas have to be entered in cells B17, B18 and B19. We shall first deal with the formula in B17. This allows us to acquaint ourselves with the structure and the fundamental procedure of working with formulas.

There are various methods of entering a formula in a table in 1-2-3/W:

(a) Constructing a formula by specifying the cell positions

You enter the formula by specifying the cell positions which are necessary for the calculation. These are linked to each other using the required operators. In order to calculate the sum of the turnovers for field B17, you must enter the following:

```
+B4+B5+B6+B7+B8+B9+B10+B11+B12+B13+B14+B15
```

When the formula has been confirmed using Enter, the correct result is shown in the B17 cell. When the cell pointer is on the cell in question the formula is shown in the Contents box of the Edit line.

(b) Constructing a formula by moving the cell pointer

Moving the cell pointer is a quicker method of specifying the cells which are necessary for the calculation. After activating the result field and pressing the plus key (+), the cell pointer can be moved over the cells which form part of the calculation. Click on the first cell and type the operator to be used, for instance the plus sign. Then move to the next cell and type the operator. When the Enter key has been pressed, the pointer will return to the result cell. In this way, a formula will be constructed identical to the one above.

(c) Constructing a formula using range names

This procedure facilitates addressing individual cells when working with individual cells and cell ranges in larger tables. We shall deal with this extensively later.

If the formula has been constructed correctly, it can be confirmed by pressing the Enter key. The result is automatically placed in the result cell which has been activated using the cell pointer. In the example in question, this result should appear as follows:

The figure shows the result in cell B17: 3556. At the same time, the corresponding formula is displayed in the Contents box on the Edit line. Formulas which are not formally correct are not accepted by 1-2-3/W. This is recognizable by the acoustic signal (peep) emitted by the computer. A common error, for example, is the entry of a space before or after an operator. In a case like this, the formula entered can be changed in the EDIT mode (F2 key) just like an erroneous result.

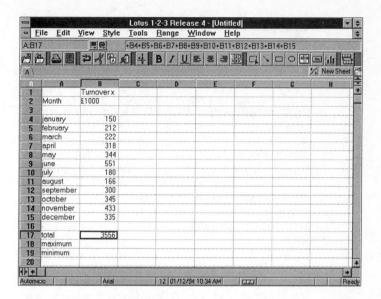

The result of a calculation formula

Different types of formulas can be constructed in 1-2-3/W. In our example, we have used an *arithmetic formula* to calculate the sum. The calculations take place using number values (numeric data) and arithmetic operators.

Another type of formula is the *text formula*. In this, the texts (labels) are linked using the string operator (&). Finally, there are the *logical formulas*. Here, values which occur in two or more cells are compared to each other using the comparison operators AND, OR, and NOT, and the result is placed in a separate cell. We shall return to this topic later.

The following checklist gives a summary of the procedures using arithmetic formulas:

■ Activate the result cell (ie. the formula cell) using the cursor keys.

■ Select the correct mode for entering formulas by pressing the plus sign.
■ Enter the formula, for example B4+B5+...
■ Confirm the input using Enter.

In order to display a cell formula later, you only have to place the cell pointer in that cell. The corresponding formula will then be shown in the Contents box of the Edit line. The *Number Format* option from the *Style* menu also provides this facility. Activate the Label option in the Format box. A global modification can be applied by selecting the *Worksheet Defaults* option from the *Style* menu and then activating the Number Format box. Select the Label option. In both cases, the cell will display the formula instead of the result.

Constructing formulas using functions

The formulas which 1-2-3/W provides can save the user a great deal of work. Among other things, there are functions for calculating the sum and for the determination of maximum and minimum values.

The general formulation of the sum function is as follows:

```
@SUM (list)
```

Using this function, you can calculate the sum of a row or column, and also the sum of numbers in random cells. In our example, you should proceed as follows:

■ Activate the result cell B17 using the cursor keys or by clicking on it.
■ Activate the function by typing the at sign (@).
■ Enter the function name: SUM.
■ Place the arguments behind it between brackets, as follows: (B4..B15).
■ Confirm the input using Enter.

If you done everything properly, the screen should look like this:

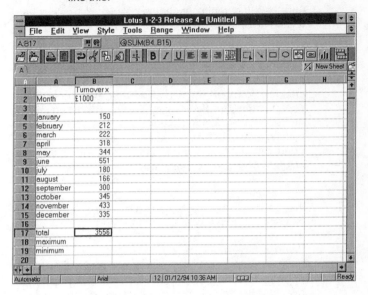

Applying the SUM function

All functions begin with an at sign. Then a key word must be specified, SUM in our example. Subsequently, the corresponding cell range should be placed between brackets. To determine the cell range, proceed as follows:

■ First specify the position of one outer (corner) cell.
■ Then type two points (the range operator).
■ Finally specify the other outermost cell.

It is also possible to specify an outer cell by moving to it using the cursor keys or the mouse.

In this way, the maximum and minimum values can be calculated using the appropriate functions: the maximum value using @MAX(list) and the minimum value using @MIN(list).

In all cases, the rule is that in the result cell first the corresponding function name, preceded by the at sign, and then the range or the values for the calculation should be entered between brackets.

Note: If you do not wish to type the function name your-self, click on the function button (with the @ symbol) on the Edit line. A list of the most commonly-used functions appears. You only need to click on SUM to activate the @SUM function. If you wish to view all functions, click on *List All*. This is particularly convenient in the case of lengthy functions. The arguments which have to be spe-cified with the function are shown in a box so that the chance of mistakes is minimized.

Note: If several arguments occur between the brackets, they should be separated by a semi-colon. For example:

```
@SUM(B4..B6;B9..B12)
```

In order to carry out our example, the exercise 'Turn-over calculation', we require the following formulas:

```
B17 = @SUM(B4..B15)
B18 = @MAX(B4..B15)
B19 = @MIN(B4..B15)
```

When all commands have been confirmed using the Enter key, the table is quickly completed.

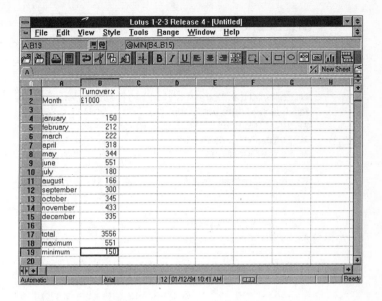

Application of the function

> *Note:* There is also an icon available in the SmartIcons set to perform the SUM function. By clicking on it, the sum function is activated immediately.

SUM function SmartIcon

> You have now become acquainted with the first group of functions provided by 1-2-3/W: the statistical functions, also called the arithmetic functions. Other functions of this type are:

> ■ average: @AVG(list)
> ■ standard deviation: @STD(list)
> ■ variance: @VAR(list)
> ■ count entries: @COUNT(list).

In addition to statistical functions, 1-2-3/W also provides the following other types of functions:

■ mathematical basic functions
■ logical functions
■ financial functions
■ date and time functions
■ string functions
■ database functions
■ special functions.

Examples of the most important functions will be dealt with later.

Summary of chapter 3

■ Before text, numbers or formulas can be entered, the cell pointer must be moved to the desired cell position. When you enter data, they also appear in the Contents box of the Edit line on the Control Panel.
■ Confirmation of values entered can take place using either Enter or the cursor keys. You can also click on the Confirm button on the Edit line.
■ The program recognizes the type of input by the character which is first entered. Input which is neither a number nor a formula is regarded as text (label). A cell can contain a maximum of 512 characters.
■ Input is checked by 1-2-3/W for formal errors. An acoustic signal is given if an error is registered. Formally correct input is stored in the currently active cell and displayed.
■ Erroneous input can be corrected immediately. Later correction can best be executed by activating the EDIT mode (F2 key) or by overwriting the old information with the new.
■ The following information can be placed in a formula: number values, strings, cell addresses, range names and @ functions. They are linked using operators.
■ The use of functions considerably simplifies the input of formulas. The @ functions contain integrated for-

mulas and enable calculations to be made with numbers and text.

■ Formulas provide the following possibilities:
- linking two or more cells in a worksheet
- automatic calculation of results
- elaborating several variants of a problem.

4   Working with files

A worksheet which has been made using 1-2-3/W is initially only in memory. If the computer is switched off,
the worksheet is irretrievably lost. Therefore, in order to
be able to use the worksheet at a later date, it has to be
stored on a permanent medium, on disk for instance.
You can then retrieve it at any required moment. The
version on disk is copied to computer working memory.
It can subsequently be edited. This chapter deals with
working with files, including saving and opening new
and already-made worksheets.

The commands which are essential for working with
files are located in the *File* menu in 1-2-3/W. When you
have activated this menu, the following screen appears:

The File menu

The commands shown here enable you to save and retrieve files and to execute other management functions
with files. The individual options are listed along with
their significance.

option	significance
New	Creates an new worksheet file and places it in the window.
Open	Activates an existing worksheet and places it in the window.
Close	Terminates working with the file in the currently active window.
Save	Saves a file which has been saved previously under a new name.
Save As	Saves a file for the first time or saves a file under another name.
Protect	Protects the current file and specifies file reservation.
Send Mail	Sends the current file or a selection from it via electronic mail.
Print Preview	Shows how the current selection will appear on paper.
Exit	This command closes your 1-2-3/W session.

The remaining options, Page Setup, Print and Print Setup will be dealt with in chapter 6.

4.1 Saving files

In the outline given below, we shall assume that the files are to be saved on the diskette in drive A:.

The *File* menu contains two commands for saving files. They are available for different reasons. In our example we shall save the file for the first time. To do this, we select the *Save As* option. The dialog box on the following page appears:

The various components of the window have the following significance:

■ A suitable name for the document must be specified in the File Name text box. You must adhere to the normal DOS conventions (a maximum of eight char-

acters, no spaces, no special characters). The extension is automatically assigned by the program: WK4.
■ The currently active directory is displayed in the Directories list. You can activate a different directory if you wish by double-clicking with the mouse or using the Tab and cursor keys and pressing Enter.
■ The Drives list contains all the available drives. You can open the list by clicking on the arrow or by using the Tab and cursor keys. You can then select a different drive.
■ The File Type list enables you to save the file in a different format if required.

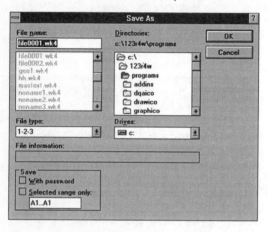

The Save As dialog window

The significance of the full file name is as follows:

Under Directories:
■ C:\ indicates that the file is to be saved on drive C:.
■ The directory and subdirectory of the drive are indicated behind the first backslash. The file is to be saved here. In our case, that is 123r4w\programs.

Under File name:
■ The worksheet file name is shown here: FILE0001.WK4. If nothing else is specified, the ex-

tension is always WK4. If you have not yet assigned a name to the file, the name FILE0001 is always initially proposed by the program. This is automatically increased by one for each subsequent file.

Normally, you would not accept this suggestion because it offers no insight into the contents of the file. Allocate a meaningful name and keep the following rules in mind:

■ A maximum of eight characters, followed by a dot and three letters for the extension if required.
■ Capitals, small letters, numbers and underlining are permitted.
■ No spaces.
■ No special (reserved) characters.

Our example deals with a file which is to be saved for the first time. This is to take place on a diskette in drive A:. We shall assign it the name TURNOVR1. When you have selected the *Save* command from the *File* menu, enter the specifications in the Save As window as shown below:

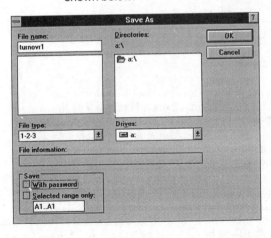

The completed Save As dialog window

Thus, the name of the worksheet is entered in the File
Name and Drive A: is selected from the Drives pull-
down list. Click on OK or activate it using the Tab key
and press Enter. The file is then saved and the name of
the file with its extension appears in the title bar of the
window.

The file remains open and is thus ready to be edited further. If that is no longer necessary, you can close it
using the *Close* option from the *File* menu.

As you see, saving a file is quite straightforward. Nevertheless, pay close attention to the following remarks:

■ The file can be stored in a particular directory by ex-
plicitly specifying the drive and directory.
■ 1-2-3/W automatically assigns an extension to a file
which indicates to which type the file belongs. In the
case of worksheet files, this is WK4.
■ If a specified file name already exists in the directory
on the disk, the following error message appears:

Error message for name conflict

You must now choose whether or not you wish to replace the old version. Choose Replace if you no longer
need the old version. Choose Backup if you wish to replace the old version with the new but you also wish to
retain a copy of the old version. This is then assigned
the extension BAK.

■ You can also save a file created under 1-2-3/W in
such a way that it can be read by the DOS version 2
of the program. In that case, specify 1-2-3 (WK1) in
the File Type box. However, this is not possible for a
protected file or a file which contains several worksheets.

4.2 Saving edited files

When saving edited files you can select one of two possibilities. You can save it under the same, existing name or under a different name.

a) **Saving under another name:** In this case, you must select the *Save As* option from the *File* menu as discussed above. Specify a different name and confirm this by pressing Enter or clicking on OK. The file is saved under a new name and the old file is retained on disk under its previous name.

b) **Under the same name:** Use this option when you no longer require the old worksheet version. Select then the *Save* option from the *File* menu. The worksheet is saved without further question.

Keep the following points in mind:

■ The *Save* command is useful if the current file already exists on disk.

■ You can also activate the Save command by clicking on the Save icon in the SmartIcons (2nd from the left).

■ The default directory in which files are saved cannot be altered if you select the *Save* option.

4.3 Saving files with a password

As an extra service, 1-2-3/W provides the facility of entering a password along with the file when saving it. In this way, you can prevent unauthorized persons activating the file. The file can then only be activated if the password is given.

To do this, activate the With Password check box in the Save group in the Save As window. Now a password has to be given when files are saved. Unauthorized persons are now unable to examine the contents of the file as long as the password is not given. Even by means of commands to the operating system it is extremely difficult to view the file contents.

Exercise 4-1: Save files with a password

Save the example file under a new name. Assign the name TURNOVR3.WK4 and allocate the password SAFETY to it.

In order to carry out this exercise, open the *Save As* dialog box and specify the name of the file: TURNOVR3.WK4. Then activate the With Password check box. See the figure below:

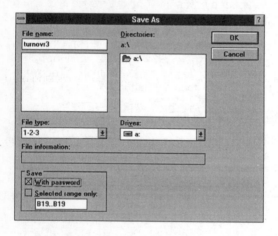

Saving a File with a password

When you have confirmed this by clicking on OK or activating OK using the Tab key and pressing Enter, the following dialog box appears:

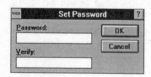

Set Password

Type the password (SAFETY) in the Password box. This word is not shown on the screen. Only asterisks are displayed, one for each letter. Press Tab and type the password again in the Verify box. When the words have been entered identically, click on OK.

Each time you attempt to open the worksheet, you will have to specify the password.

The following summary outlines the steps once more:

■ Open the *File* menu using Alt-F or by clicking on the menu name.
■ Select the *Save As* option.
■ Type the name of the file.
■ Activate the With Password check box by clicking on it or by pressing Alt-W.
■ Type the password in the text box: SAFETY.
■ Press Tab or click on the Verify box. Repeat the password.
■ Confirm the input using Enter or click on OK.

■ The password may consist of a maximum of fifteen letters. Spaces, capitals and small letters are allowed.
■ If the letters entered in the Verify box do not fully correspond to those in the Password box an error message will appear to indicate this. You must take into account the precise notation in terms of capitals and small letters.

A password can always be revoked later. To do this, you must first open the file and then select the *Save As* option from the *File* menu. Remove the cross in the With Password box by clicking on it or by pressing Alt-W. When you have confirmed this, the file is no longer protected by the password.

4.4   Saving part of the worksheet

It is also possible to save only a part of the worksheet instead of saving it all. By extracting the required data, a smaller file can be created out of the total file. This can be convenient, for instance, if you wish to split a large file into smaller files in order to save it on different diskettes.

Exercise 4-2:

Select the *Save As* option from the *File* menu. Activate the Selected Range Only check box in the Save group. You can then specify the range you wish to save in the text box underneath.

Here is a summary of the file saving procedure:

action	**menu/command**
Saving for the first time	File, Save or File, Save As
Saving an edited file	
a) under the same name	File, Save
b) under a new name	File, Save As
Saving with password	File, Save As and activate With Password check box
Saving part of a file	File, Save As and activate Selected Range Only

4.5   Closing a file and opening a new worksheet

In order to open a new worksheet, it is sometimes necessary to clear the worksheet area to make space for the new worksheet. In that case, the previous worksheet has to be closed properly.

The contents of the working memory are removed by means of the *Close* command in the *File* menu. The work area is then freed for the next task. If the previous file has not yet been saved, the program provides the opportunity to do so. This prevents a worksheet being lost unintentionally.

4.6 Opening existing files

If you wish to edit a file which has been saved previously, a copy of it has to be loaded from disk into working memory. The file is retained on disk.

In 1-2-3/W, a file is opened by means of the *Open* command from the *File* menu.

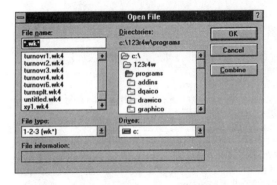

The Open File dialog window

The components of the Open File window are as follows:

option	significance
File name	The name of the file to be opened should be typed here. You may also select the name from the file list underneath.
Directories	List of directories. Select the directory containing the required file.

File type   Use this box to open a file which has
                          been saved in a different file format.

Drives   Drop-down list of drives from which
                          you can select the required file.

File Information   Displays information about the se-
                          lected file: date and time when last
                          edited, file size.

You must first specify the name of the file. That can be
done by typing the name, if known, on the keyboard. But
it is also possible to make a selection from the file list. If
the required file does not appear in this list, select the
appropriate directory or drive from the other lists. The
currently active directory is shown in the dialog window.

If, for instance, you wish to open the TURNOVR1.WK4
file again, proceed as follows:

- Open the *File* menu using Alt-F or by clicking on the
  menu name.
- Select the *Open* command.
- Type the file name, along with the directory if re-
  quired: A:TURNOVR1.WK4.
- Press Enter or click on OK.

The required worksheet appears on the screen. The cell
pointer is located at the same position as it was when
the worksheet was saved.

Specifying a file name can take place in various ways:

**The file name can be typed in the File Name text
box.** The name must correspond exactly to the name
given when the file was saved (capitals or small letters
make no difference here). Normally it is not necessary
to specify an extension.

**The file name can also be selected from the file list
underneath File Name.** The names of the files in the
currently active directory appear in alphabetical order in
the list. It is occasionally necessary to select the appropriate drive containing the required directory first. The

file is then activated by clicking on it or by moving to it using the cursor keys. Confirm using OK.

When opening files which are safeguarded with a password, a window first appears in which you must specify the correct password. It must be specified exactly in terms of capitals and small letters.

4.7 Activating several files

1-2-3/W is able to open several files simultaneously. This has the following advantages:

- Data from different files can be easily linked.
- It is possible to work with one file while a macro performs a task in another file, executing a print job for instance.
- Formulas which are relevant to data and ranges in other files can easily be adopted into a current file.

Worksheet files which are loaded in program memory are referred to as *opened files*. One of these files is readily available, the *active file*. It is possible to switch between files by means of the *Window* menu (see the figure below).

The Window menu

All opened files are shown in the lower part of this menu, in this case the files TURNOVR1.WK4 and TUR-NOVR3.WK4. A maximum of nine opened windows can be shown in this menu. A tick is located in front of the currently active file.

Normally, only the currently active file is shown in the foreground. If another file is activated, this covers the first file. This situation can be altered by selecting the *Tile* option from the *Window* menu. The window than appears as follows:

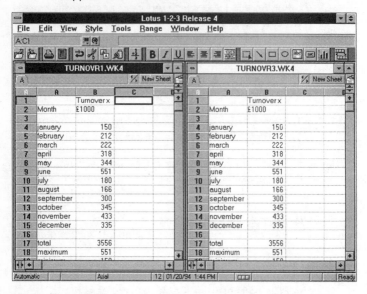

Adjacent windows

This display can be altered by clicking on the maximize button of the window which is to appear on its own on the screen.

4.8   Special cases when working with files

Under 1-2-3/W, there are special regulations for cases in which several people have to work with files simultaneously. This involves:

■ access control
■ protection of the files against modification in simultaneous reading situations.

The following options are available for these cases:

File, Protect	Protects the currently active file and determines the File reservation settings.
Edit, Links, *Link Type, File Links*	Calculates the relevant formulas in the active files which apply to the linked files.

Determining the File reservation

The reservation of created files must always be individually regulated if several users are working on one computer or are working simultaneously in a network or multi-user computer system. To do this, activate the appropriate dialog window by selecting *Protect* from the *File* menu.

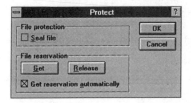

Specifying File reservation

In this, you can define a file reservation for each file in order to ensure that only authorized users are able to make modifications to the file. The Get Reservation Automatically check box determines that the reservation is automatically assigned when the file is opened.

Protecting files against alteration

File data can also be protected in such a way that other users are able to examine the file contents but are unable to make changes to these. This is done by placing a cross in the Seal File check box. Then select OK. You will be asked to specify and verify a password. Enter these and press Enter. The file is protected against

changes. This situation can only be altered by removing
the cross from the Seal File box. You must specify the
correct password in order to do so.

Summary of chapter 4

- A file is stored on disk(ette) by means of the *Save*
  command from the *File* menu. The file name must
  then be entered if this has not yet been done. The file
  can be protected by allocating a password.
- An existing worksheet can be edited by opening it
  using the *Open* command from the *File* menu. It then
  appears on the screen.
- When you have completed working on the file, you
  can close it using the *Close* command from the *File*
  menu. The file is removed from the screen and
  cleared from working memory.
- It is possible to display several files adjacently on the
  screen at one time. This is done by means of the *Tile*
  command from the *Window* menu. This menu also
  shows all currently opened files.
- In cases where several users are working in the program, access to the files is controlled by means of the
  Protect command from the *File* menu.

5 Extending, designing and editing worksheets

Information and calculations in a worksheet tend to be identical in many areas of the worksheet. In that case, copying is a useful way of extending the worksheet.

It is, of course, important to retain a clear overview of the information in large worksheets. 1-2-3/W provides various layout options for the display of numbers and texts (such as alignment) and the emphasis of cells (borders, colour, shadow).

This chapter also discusses how to to get to grips effectively with editing worksheets.

5.1 Copying cell contents

We shall now extend the TURNOVR1.WK4 worksheet. Here, the command COPY can be extremely useful in saving a great deal of input work. The following example will make this clear:

Exercise 5-1: Extending a worksheet by copying

Next to the second column in the original worksheet, another column is to be created in which the percentage of the turnover per month is to be registered.

a) First open the TURNOVR1.WK4 worksheet.
b) Enter the title of the column in column C. Then enter the formula in cell C4 and enter the figures for the other months into the cells underneath.
c) Save the worksheet under the name TURN-OVR2.WK4.

The result of the new worksheet should eventually appear as shown:

Month	Turnover x £1000	Share in %
january	150	4.2
february	212	6.0
march	222	6.2
april	318	8.9
may	344	9.7
june	551	15.5
july	180	5.1
august	166	4.7
september	300	8.4
october	345	9.7
november	433	12.2
december	335	9.4
total	3556	
maximum	551	
minimum	150	

5.1.1   Copy possibilities

In order to save unnecessary input work, 1-2-3/W provides the possibility of copying the contents of cells. This may be done with texts, numbers and formulas.

With *texts* (labels) and *numbers* (known values) an exact duplication is made of the original data for another cell or cells.

If you wish to copy *formulas*, it is possible for the program to adjust the cell addresses automatically. It is important here to specify the cell addresses correctly and you must keep in mind the difference between relative, absolute and mixed cell addresses. More information about these is given below.

When copying, you make use of the *Copy* command in the *Edit* menu. Before giving the command, you must activate, using the cell pointer, the cell or range of cells to be copied. Subsequently, having selected the *Copy* command, the target range must be specified. Then select the *Paste* command from the *Edit* menu in order to transmit the copied data to the target range.

If you are working in windows with various worksheets (more about this later), you can copy from one worksheet window to another. In that case, you must activate the target file in the *Window* menu, activate the target range in the other window and then select the *Paste* command from the *Edit* menu.

5.1.2 Copying formulas

It is useful to be able to copy a formula if the same calculation has to be made repeatedly in certain row or column.
In our example dealing with turnover, it is advisable, for example, to enter the formula in cell C4 first and to copy it from there to the cells C5 to C15. The calculation of the percentage in the turnover remains the same for each month. Thus, it is not necessary to enter the formula in each individual cell.

First, the formula has to be constructed in cell C4 for the month of January. This is as follows:

```
+B4*100/B17
```

When the command is confirmed, the share is immediately calculated.

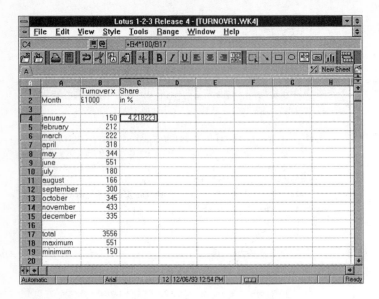

The formula in C4

You will observe that the result displays as many places behind the decimal point as the column width allows. The formula which has been entered in cell C4 must now be copied eleven times for the remaining months. To do this, activate the source range (C4) and then select the *Copy* command from the *Edit* menu. When you have selected the target range by dragging the cell pointer from C5 to C15 (or hold down Shift and press Cursor Down), select the *Paste* command from the *Edit* menu.

Thus, a formula is copied as follows:

- Activate the cell which is to be copied by clicking on it or by moving to it using the cursor keys. .
- Select the *Copy* command from the *Edit* menu (Alt-E, C).
- Specify the target range by dragging the cell pointer from C5 to C15 using the mouse or Shift-Cursor Down.

■ Select the *Paste* command from the *Edit* menu (Alt-E, P).

The following screen is the result:

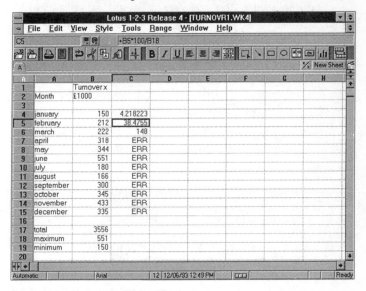

The screen after Copy and Paste

The figure shows that we have made an error somewhere. This is due to the fact that we have not taken into consideration the difference between absolute and relative addresses. In principle, *1-2-3/W addresses the cells in a relative way*. This means that, when copying, the cell position is always determined relative to the copy direction. This means that the copy adopted into another cell is no longer completely or exactly derived from the original formula.

If you place the cell pointer on one of the cells indicating ERR, you will get an idea of what has gone wrong. The relative cell address is correct for the cell containing the monthly turnover. In this way, when copying the formula, the cells for the range of months, B5, B6 etc. are addressed as you would wish. However, the total turnover, the sum in cell B17, is different. The reference point of the formula, in the example, must always be exactly cell B17. This cell address must not move downwards as it does when the turnover cells are addressed. The monthly turnovers must all be compared to B17. Accordingly, B17 must be addressed absolutely. To do this, it is necessary to enter a dollar sign before the specification of the column and row B17. The formula will then appear as follows:

```
B4*100/$B$17
```

When addressing cells, the following variants can be distinguished:

variant	**effect/example**
Relative address	The cell address is determined by a relative cell address. Example: the monthly turnover.
Absolute address	The cell address in the copy is identical to that specified in the original formula. Example: SUM $B$8
Mixed cell address	- Relative column, absolute row. Example:B$8
	- Absolute column, relative row. Example: $B8.

Thus, the method of cell addressing can be influenced as follows:

■ By means of a dollar sign in front of the column or row. The dollar sign makes the addressing absolute.
■ By means of the F4 function key. First place the cell pointer on the cell containing the formula or on the Contents box of the Edit line. Each time you press F4 you switch to another of the four forms of cell addressing. (If you have more than one worksheet in the file, the Tab letter of the worksheet will also be

shown. This enables you to copy formulas to other worksheets.)

1-2-3/W always addresses cells relatively, in principle. The address becomes absolute only when the dollar sign is specified. For those who find it too much work to specify the dollar signs, there is an alternative. When the appropriate cell has been activated using the cell pointer, you only need to activate the ABS function using the function key F4. In this way, an absolute address is specified. This function can be cancelled by pressing F4 once more.

Summarizing:

absolute cell address	**relative cell address**
The cell address in the copy must correspond to the original	The cell address is determined by the relative position
The sum, in our example	The monthly turnover, in our example
$B$17	B4

If you now repeat the *Copy* command having entered the correct formula in cell C4, the screen will appear as shown on the following page.

Finally, save this worksheet under the name TURN-OVR2.

In fact, when addressing the annual turnover, only the row needed to be addressed absolutely. The column could have retained its relative address. Thus, the dollar sign in front of the B was not really necessary. In this case, we are dealing with a mixed address, since only one of the factors, column or row, receives a dollar sign. In our example the result still remains the same. However, there is an advantage to mixed reference. For instance, if we should add a column containing real turn-over values, this formula could be copied directly.

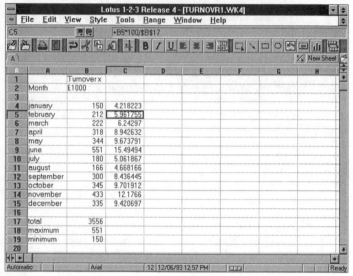

The screen with the corrected formula

5.2   Worksheet layout

The previous figure shows that the calculated percent-ages are displayed as precisely as possible, depending on the column width. However, this is not always orderly or necessary. The format can be altered if required. This also applies to the layout of the cell data.

5.2.1   Aligning cell data

As previously mentioned, 1-2-3/W left-aligns the labels (texts) in the cells and right-aligns the numbers. As we have seen, this layout can be altered using the *Work-sheet Defaults* option from the *Style* menu.

However, this can also be done specifically for individual cells in a worksheet. The possibilities are Left, Right and Center. To do this, open the *Style* menu and select the *Alignment* option. The following dialog window appears:

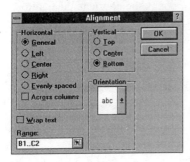

Alignment dialog box

In our example, we shall right-align the text data in columns B and C in order to have them align with the number values in these columns. Proceed as follows:

- Activate, using the mouse or Shift-Cursor, the range which is to be re-aligned, here B1..C2.
- Open the *Style* menu, using Alt-S or by clicking on the menu name.
- Select the *Alignment* option (press A or click on it).
- Select Right (press R or click on the options button).
- Confirm using Enter or click on OK.

The result is shown in the figure on the following page. The text data in the specified range are now aligned to the numbers underneath.

You will have noticed that when the cell pointer is positioned on one of the cells in the range which has just been re-aligned, each text label in the Contents box now has a prefix. This prefix refers to the way in which the text is aligned. In our example, inverted commas are located where the apostrophe used to be up until now. The various prefixes have particular significance.

sign	meaning
' apostrophe	left-aligned
" inverted commas	right-aligned
^ caret	centred
\ backslash	repeat; the character is inserted in the cell until the cell is full
I vertical stripe	the data line in the first column of a range to be printed is not reproduced

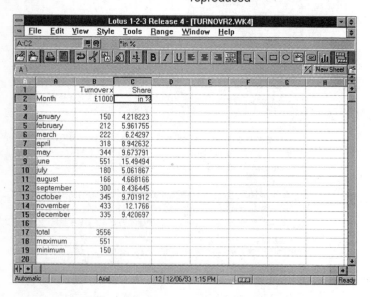

The screen after right-alignment

If you wish to have a different form of alignment than normal, you can specify the appropriate sign when making the input. This is not reproduced in the cell itself in the worksheet. It is only shown in the Contents box on the Edit line when the cell pointer is located in the corresponding cell.

Placing a format sign is especially important in the following cases:

■ a text which begins with a number: '031 Edinburgh
■ a text which begins with an operator: '+17.5% VAT.

If the prefix is not specified, the program will not accept
the input in cases such as these.

A prefix may also be changed. In that case, place the
cell pointer on the label cell and press F2, the EDIT key.
Using the cursor keys, you can now move to the prefix
and make the alteration.

Use of the backslash is very handy if characters in a cell
have to be repeated. An extended line, for example, can
be made by pressing the backslash and one underlining
sign:

_

The result of this is that the whole cell is underlined.

Tip: Use the SmartIcons to alter the alignment of data in
cells. Click on the appropriate icon while the relevant
cell is active. The alteration is made immediately.

5.2.2   Specifying the numbers format

The previous example has indicated that it is possible to
have a large amount of figures behind the decimal
point. Fifteen is the maximum. The number format can
also be changed, although the format does not influence the number stored in the 1-2-3/W memory. The
internal accuracy remains the same regardless of the
display on the screen.

In order to change the number format to two digits behind the point, you should proceed as follows: Select
the *Number Format* option from the *Style* menu.

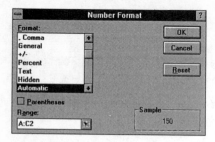

The Number Format dialog box

The options have the following significance:

format	example	function
Fixed	4.2	Fixed number of digits (here 1) behind the decimal point, maximum of 15
Scientific	-4.3E+01	Exponential, scientific notation
Currency	£9.99	Adds currency symbol to the value (in front or behind)
Comma	1,000	Thousands separator
General	4.178	Real numbers, meaningless zeros behind the decimal point omitted
+/-	++++++	Symbol display (bar chart)
Percent	4.178%	Adds percent sign
Text	+C5-D5	Displays the formula as text not as calculated value
Hidden		Suppresses display of data
Automatic		The 1-2-3/W default settings

Label		All input, even numbers, is regarded as text
		44+2 remains as such
Date	10/11	Various (5) methods of displaying the date
Time	20:00	Various (4) methods of displaying the time

The Reset button enables you to restore the original settings after alteration.

In our example, we wish to limit the percentages to one digit behind the decimal point. To do this, the standard settings should be altered using the Fixed option in the Format group. Proceed as follows:

■ Select the range C4..C15 using Shift-Cursor Down or using the mouse.
■ Open the *Style* menu by clicking on it or pressing Alt-S.
■ Select the *Number Format* option in order to open the dialog window.
■ Activate the Fixed option and move to the Decimal Places box by clicking on it with the mouse or by pressing Tab. Specify the number of digits behind the decimal point: 1.
■ Confirm the values entered by pressing Enter.

This produces the required format in the selected cells.

Save the worksheet under the name TURNOVR2.WK4.

Formatting ranges

Individual formatting of each cell is very laborious if the intention is to format a group of cells (a row or column). Accordingly, 1-2-3/W provides the possibility of marking a range before the command is chosen. But in most dialog windows there is also the opportunity of defining a range to which the chosen command is to apply. This saves a great deal of work in situations like these. Being able to specify ranges makes working with spreadsheets a good deal easier.

In this context, the term **range** refers to a rectangular block of cells which belong together. This can be:

- a (part of a) column
- a (part of a) row
- a block containing several (parts of) rows and columns.

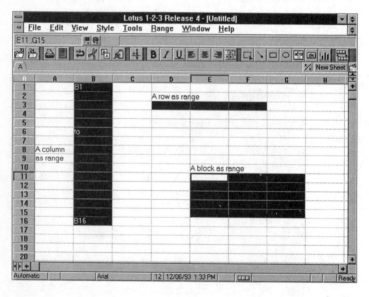

Worksheet ranges

There are various ways of specifying a range in 1-2-3/W:

When you have chosen the command:
- by specifying the cell addresses in the Range text box. This means specifying the top left-hand corner cell and the lower right-hand corner cell of the required range, separated from each other by two points.
- by activating the cells using the cell pointer. Activate the Range box (click on it or press Alt-A). Move to the first cell of the range using the mouse or the cursor keys. The dialog box has disappeared for the moment. Drag the mouse over the required range or press Shift-Cursor Keys to select the range. When you release the mouse or the Shift key, the dialog window reappears. The selected range is shown in the Range text box.
- by using range names (more about this later).

Prior to choosing the command:
- Select the range by dragging the mouse over the relevant cells or by using Shift-Cursor Keys.

5.2.3   Altering the font and font size

In addition to the *Alignment* option outlined above, the *Style* menu contains several other interesting options dealing with the appearance of the worksheet. These can be used to, for instance, apply certain fonts to the headings in a worksheet, to introduce separating lines between certain parts of the worksheet or to clearly distinguish the input data from the calculated results.

The following exercise will be used to illustrate the use of fonts.

Exercise 5-2: Using different fonts in a worksheet

First open the TURNOVR2.WK4 worksheet and make the following modifications to the lettering:

a) Increase the size of the font in the range A1..C2 to, for instance, 14 point Arial.

b) The range A17..B19 is to be allocated 12 point Times New Roman. This is also to be in boldface.

c) Save the result under the name TURNOVR4.WK4.

Procedure: Open the TURNOVR2.WK4 worksheet and also open the *Style* menu. Select the *Font & Attributes* option. The following dialog window appears:

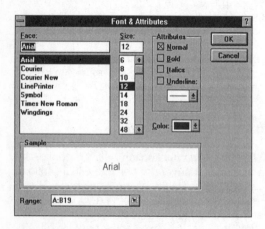

Font & Attributes dialog window

This window enables you to define fonts for both the whole worksheet and for particular parts of it.

■ Select the required font from the Face list.
■ Specify the range to which the font is to apply, if you did not select a range in advance.

There are three attributes which can be allocated to a font: Bold, Italics and Underline. The text in the selected range then acquires the specified attribute(s).

Determining the font

The dialog box shows that various fonts are available. Select one of the font sets from the list. (Move to the list by clicking on it or press Tab and cursor keys.) You can specify the font size and the attributes by moving to the appropriate boxes (click or Tab) and making the desired selection (click or cursor keys). The Sample box gives an example of your choice. When you activate OK (click or press Enter) the font set is adapted as you have specified.

Allocating the selected font to a worksheet range

The exercise can be carried out by first selecting the range to which you wish the font to apply: A1..C2. Then select *Font & Attributes* from the *Style* menu. Adopt the settings from the figure shown below:

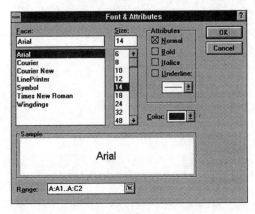

Settings in Font & Attributes window

When you press Enter or click on OK, the alterations
are applied to the worksheet range.

Thus, the procedure is as follows:

- Select the range to which the alterations are to be ap-
  plied.
- Select *Font & Attributes* from the *Style* menu.
- Highlight the required font by clicking, or using Tab
  and cursor keys.
- Select the required size from the Size box (click or
  Tab, cursor).
- If you have not already selected the range, you can
  specify the range in the Range box.
- Execute the command by pressing Enter or clicking
  on OK.

The layout of the result data can be altered in a similar
manner. The worksheet will then look something like
this:

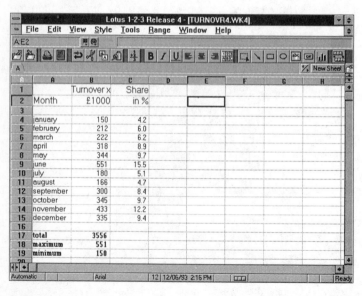

The new worksheet layout

5.2.4   Adding lines and borders

The attractiveness of your worksheets can be increased by means of lines and frames.

Exercise 5-3: Add borders to certain areas of the worksheet

Open the worksheet which you edited and saved under the name TURNOVR4.WK4. Make the following adjustments:

a) The top of the worksheet is to be enclosed by a thick frame. Create the following lines:
   A1..A2 left
   A1..C1 top
   C1..C2 right
   A2..C2 bottom
b) In the result range C4..C15, each cell is to be given a border.
c) Under row 15 a line is to be drawn A15..C15.
d) Save the worksheet under the name TURN-OVR4.WK4.

The *Lines & Color* option from the *Style* menu is available to perform these tasks. Select this option.

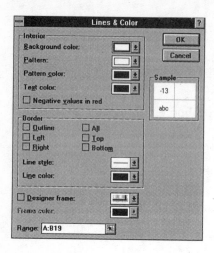

To cope with our exercise, we require the options from the Border box. These have the following significance:

option	significance
Outline	Draws a thin border around the selected range.
Left	Draws a vertical line at the left-hand side of the cell.
Right	Draws a vertical line at the right-hand side of the cell.
All	Assigns an individual border to each cell in the selected range.
Top	Draws a horizontal line at the top of the cell.
Bottom	Draws a horizontal line at the bottom of the cell.

Activate the required option by placing a cross in the check box. The Line Style drop-down options list is located in the same group. This enables you to determine the thickness and the type of line you wish to apply. The Line Color drop-down list defines the colour of the line.

When you have made the required modifications, the worksheet has the following appearance:

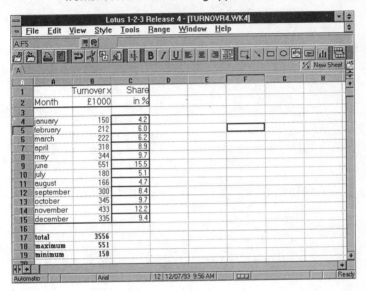

Worksheet with lines and borders

5.2.5 Allocating colours to cells

The *Lines & Color* option from the *Style* menu enables you to allocate colours to certain parts of your worksheet. This applies to text (contents of a cell), the background and the number format. The relevant options are located in the Interior group within the *Lines & Color* dialog window.

The options have the following significance:

option	significance
Background color	Defines the background colour for a range
Pattern	Defines the background pattern for a range
Pattern color	Defines a colour for the background pattern
Text color	Defines the colour for a text
Negative values in red	Negative values are displayed in red

The last option accentuates any negative values in a worksheet (for those who may require a daily dose of despair).

Exercise 5-4: Allocate colour to cells and shadow to the background

Open the TURNOVR4.WK4 worksheet and make the following modifications:

a) The names of the months are to be displayed in blue.

b) The background of the range A1..C2 is to be displayed in yellow and the text in this range in red.

c) The range B17..B19 is to be given a slight shadow.

d) Save the worksheet under the name TURN-COL4.WK4.

The Background color option also enables you to assign a sort of shadow to a specified range. Select one of the grey tints at the right-hand side of the colour chart.

5.3   Editing and extending worksheets

Various situations may make it necessary to edit an existing worksheet. This may require the following manoeuvres:

- adding rows or columns
- removing rows or columns
- relocating rows or columns
- altering cell data.

Exercise 5-5: Editing worksheets

Extend the worksheet in our example to include real turnover values alongside the estimated values. In addition, another column should be included to show the difference between the estimated and the real turnover.

The final result should appear as follows. Save the worksheet as TURNOVR4 and again as TURNOVR5 (we shall use the latter in an exercise in chapter 11).

Month	Estimated turnover x £1000	Share in %	Real turnover x £1000	Share in %	Difference est.- real x £1000
january	150	4.2	132	3.9	-18
february	212	6.0	260	7.6	48
march	222	6.2	322	9.4	100
april	318	8.9	312	9.2	-6
may	344	9.7	322	9.4	-22
june	551	15.5	457	13.4	-94
july	180	5.1	234	6.9	54
august	166	4.7	239	7.0	73
september	300	8.4	234	6.9	-66
october	345	9.7	317	9.3	-28
november	433	12.2	345	10.1	-88
december	335	9.4	234	6.9	-101
total	3556	3408			
maximum	551	457			
minimum	150	132			

5.3.1   Inserting rows and columns

If a worksheet has to be edited at a later date, it may occur that extra rows or columns have to be added. Space can be created in the worksheet for extra data.

We shall edit the worksheet TURNOVR4. This is loaded using the *Open* command from the *File* menu.

Inserting rows

To include the appropriate titles above the columns, a new row must be inserted at the top of the worksheet. Place the cell pointer at the position where the new row is to come (A1). Then open the *Edit* menu and select the *Insert* command. The following dialog box appears:

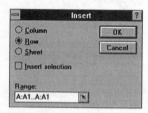

The Insert dialog box

The options in this box have the following significance:

option	significance
Column	Insert one or more columns in the currently active worksheet.
Row	Insert one or more rows in the currently active worksheet.
Sheet	Insert another worksheet. For more information about this option, refer to chapter 7 *Three-dimensional worksheets*. The new worksheet contains no data as yet.

If you specify Sheet, the following options become available:

Before	Insert the column/row/sheet before the specified position.
After	Insert the column/row/sheet after the specified position.
Quantity	Insert the specified number of columns/rows/sheets.

Rows are inserted using the Row option. When the command has been implemented, the screen will look like this:

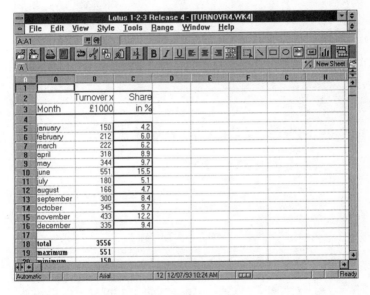

Inserted row

Now the former worksheet can be supplemented with new data:

- text data in the rows 1-3
- the real figures are placed in column D
- formulas are placed in columns E and F.

This action and the addition of data produces the following screen (note the right-aligned columns). We have adjusted the column width to 12 for the figure:

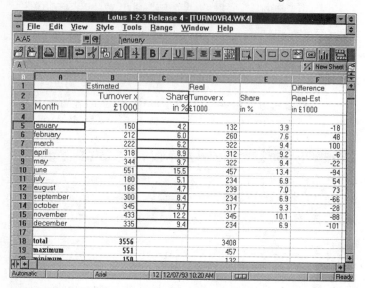

Comparison of Estimated and Real Turnover

Inserting columns

Columns are inserted in the same way as rows. Open the *Edit* menu and select the *Insert* command. Select Column by clicking or by moving the cursor.

Normally, the insertion of columns takes place as follows:

- Place the cell pointer at the position where the column is to be inserted.
- Open the *Edit* menu and select *Insert* (click or Alt-E, I).
- Select Column (click or press C). The column which has already been selected is shown in the Range

box. You can change this by clicking on a different
column if required (first click on the Range box).
■ Press Enter or click on OK to implement the command.

5.3.2   Removing rows and columns

It is, of course, possible to subsequently remove rows
and columns when they are no longer necessary. Use
the *Delete* command from the *Edit* menu. The following
menu appears:

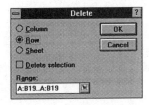

The Delete dialog box

The options in this box have the following significance:

option	significance
Column	Removes one or more columns from the currently active worksheet.
Row	Removes one or more rows from the currently active worksheet.
Sheet	Removes a worksheet if there are several worksheets in the file.

The Row option is the default selection.

The space which becomes available when rows or columns are removed is immediately filled up.

5.3.3   Moving cells

The *Cut* and *Paste* options from the *Edit* menu enable
you to move the contents of a cell or cells to a different,
specified position in the worksheet. The procedure is as
follows:

- Select the cell to be moved using the mouse or using
  the (Shift-)cursor keys.
- Select the *Cut* option from the *Edit* menu.
- Specify the target range using the mouse or the cur-
  sor keys.
- Select *Paste* from the *Edit* menu.

When the command has been implemented, the specified cells are located at the new position in the worksheet. If any data are located in the taget range, these
are removed during the copying process. Formulas in
copied cells are automatically adjusted. Thus, the func-
tional relationship between cells is retained.

5.3.4   Switching rows and columns

The *Transpose* option from the *Range* menu enables
you to copy data within a worksheet, or to a destination
outside the worksheet, and to switch rows and columns
in the process.

For instance, within a worksheet you can specify the
columns in a range as rows, and the rows as columns.
During this process, the range is copied to a new position and then switched. The rows in a range become the
columns in the destination range and the columns
become the new rows.

5.3.5   Altering data in a cell

If an alteration in numeric values takes place, the related cells are automatically recalculated. You can test
this in the example by changing the estimated turnover

for the month of June from 551 to 777 for instance. The result is then as follows:

	B	C	D	E	F
	Estimated		Real		Difference
	Turnover x	Share	Turnover x	Share	Real-Est
Month	£1000	in %	£1000	in %	in £1000
january	150	4.0	132	3.9	-18
february	212	5.6	260	7.6	48
march	222	5.9	322	9.4	100
april	318	8.4	312	9.2	-6
may	344	9.1	322	9.4	-22
june	777	20.5	457	13.4	-320
july	180	4.8	234	6.9	54
august	166	4.4	239	7.0	73
september	300	7.9	234	6.9	-66
october	345	9.1	317	9.3	-28
november	433	11.4	345	10.1	-88
december	335	8.9	234	6.9	-101
total	3782		3408		
maximum	777		457		
minimum	150		132		

Altering cell data

The figure shows that all related values have been re-calculated. These are:

- the total value of the sum and the maximum value in column B.
- all values in column C.
- the difference between estimated and real turnover in cell F10.

This recalculation is, of course, only executed if the automatic recalculation setting has been activated (*Tools, User Setup, Recalculation*).

Restore the original value for the month of June and specify the column width as 9 again.

5.4   Working with names

The usage of range names can be very important when constructing formulas, especially in large worksheets. Instead of matter-of-fact co-ordinates, names can be used. As well as being informative, it also makes it more convenient to work with cells or cell ranges. It also makes it more easy to create links with other worksheets and to specify numeric values to the graphic module.

Exercise 5-6: Allocate names to ranges in a worksheet

Open the TURNOVR2.WK4 worksheet. We shall use this worksheet to examine how names are allocated and how they are used when working with formulas. Execute the following instructions:

a) Allocate the following names to ranges in the worksheet:
   Turnover to the range B4..B15
   Share to the range C4..C15.
b) Then use the name 'Share' in the sum formula in cell C17.
c) Save the worksheet under the name TURNOVR6.

In 1-2-3/W, names are allocated using the *Name* option from the *Range* menu. To allocate the names in our example, proceed as follows:

■ Select the range B4..B15 using the mouse or Shift-Cursor Down.
■ Select the *Name* option from the *Range* menu using Alt-R, N or by clicking on it.
■ Type the name 'Turnover' in the Name dialog box.
■ Allocate the name by selecting the Add button (click with the mouse or use the Tab key).
■ Confirm by pressing Enter or clicking on OK.

When the fourth step has been performed, the dialog box will appear as shown on the following page.

The Name dialog box

When allocating a name to a range, keep the following rules in mind:

■ Names must begin with a letter.
■ Names must not contain spaces or hyphens.
■ Letters, numbers, dots and underlining are allowed.

Now assign the name 'Share' to the range C4..C15. When you have done this, you will notice that the range names will be immediately applied in the existing formulas in B17, B18 and B19. Place the cell pointer on B17 and you will be able to see that this is the case. In the Contents box of the Edit line, the following formula is displayed:

@SUM(TURNOVER)

You can do the same for the sum formula of the share. Go to cell C17 and specify the following formula:

@SUM(SHARE)

The value is shown in cell C17.

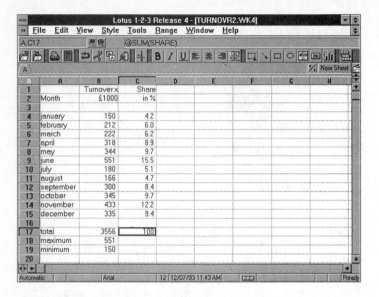

Worksheet after range name allocation

Summarizing, working with range names is particularly interesting when there is frequent reference to a certain range in a worksheet. The range name, if carefully chosen, is easier to apply in formulas than exact addressing by means of the cursor keys or cell co-ordinates.

5.5   Exercise

Development of the apprenticeship scheme

A large industrial company is interesting in developing its apprenticeship system further with respect to the choice of pupils. The exercise consists of visualizing this development and carrying out various calculations. The information and figures are to be presented in a list.

job	1990	1991	1992	1993	total
comm. adm.	123	143	154	139	559
assist. comm. adm.	87	76	128	98	389
assist. comm. sales	145	132	122	135	534
assist. mechanic	234	254	266	270	1024
lab.techn.	453	421	432	409	1715
craftsmen	211	234	267	344	1056
total	1253	1260	1369	1395	5277
average	208.8	210.0	228.2	232.5	879.5
comm. share	28.3	27.9	29.5	26.7	28.1

The exercise is carried out in the following stages:

(a) Entering text and number values.
(b) Constructing formulas for the calculation of the totals and averages and for the share of commercial staff.
(c) Formatting the average values and share with one place behind the decimal point.
(d) Saving the worksheet under the name APPRENT.

Procedures

(a) Mark the range A1..F1. Choose *style, Fonts & Attributes, Bold.* Click on OK. The text data should be placed in the first column and in cell F1. Make the first column a little wider in order to make meaningful, legible abbreviations. Use the *Column Width* option from the *Style* menu to set the width to 15 for instance. Then enter the names in the worksheet, beginning at A3. The numbers should be entered in the columns B to E, in the rows 3 to 12.

(b) For the formulas we shall make use of the @SUM and @AVE functions. This concerns the following formulas:

```
B10: @SUM(B3..B8)
B11: @AVE(B3..B8)
```

```
B12: @SUM(B3..B5)/B10*100
F3: @SUM(B3..E3)
```

The formula in B10 can be copied to cells C10..F10.
The formula in B11 can be copied to cells C11..F11.
The formula in B12 can be copied to cells C12..F12.
The formula in F3 can be copied to cell F4..F10.

(c) When you have activated cell B11 using the cell
pointer, you can specify the number of places behind
the decimal point (1 in this case) using the *Number
Format* from the *Style* menu. Select Fixed in the subsequent dialog box and choose 1 Decimal place from
the relevant box. Then specify the range B11..F12 in
the Range box.

(d) Save the worksheet under the name APPRENT
using the File Save command.

The worksheet should look like this:

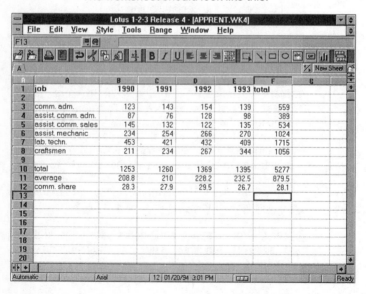

	A	B	C	D	E	F	G
1	job	1990	1991	1992	1993	total	
2							
3	comm. adm.	123	143	154	139	559	
4	assist. comm. adm.	87	76	128	98	389	
5	assist. comm. sales	145	132	122	135	534	
6	assist. mechanic	234	254	266	270	1024	
7	lab. techn.	453	421	432	409	1715	
8	craftsmen	211	234	267	344	1056	
9							
10	total	1253	1260	1369	1395	5277	
11	average	208.8	210	228.2	232.5	879.5	
12	comm. share	28.3	27.9	29.5	26.7	28.1	
13							
14							
15							
16							
17							
18							
19							
20							

Summary of chapter 5

■ Much time can be saved by copying cell contents. Numbers and formulas can be copied, in addition to text.

■ The *Copy* option from the *Edit* menu enables you to copy data. The selected source range is copied to the specified target range.

■ When copying texts and numbers, an exact duplicate of the original data is reproduced at the new position.

■ When copying formulas, you must take into account absolute and relative cell addresses.

■ It is also possible to copy the values of formulas.

■ When data is being laid out, the default settings or the settings specified in the *Worksheet Defaults* dialog window are applied. It is possible to make individual modifications.

■ The *Alignment* option from the *Style* menu enables you to align separate cells or ranges containing data in a preferred style. This can be left, right or centred.

■ The *Number Format* option from the *Style* menu enables you to alter the display of numbers in cells.

■ It is possible to insert rows and columns into worksheets. This is done by means of the *Insert* option from the *Edit* menu.

■ The *Delete* command from the *Edit* menu enables you to remove rows and columns from a worksheet.

■ The *Cut* and *Paste* options from the *Edit* menu enable you to move ranges containing data to another worksheet section.

■ An alteration to a cell leads to automatic recalculation of relevant formulas.

6   Printing worksheets

This chapter deals with how created worksheets can be printed. In this, the type of printer is largely responsible for the way in which the worksheet is eventually reproduced on paper.

The following options from the *File* menu have an effect upon the printouts:

Option	**significance/application**
Print Preview	Provides an example on screen of how the worksheet will look on the page; this applies to the specified range.
Page Setup	Determines edges, margins, headers and footers and special print options.
Print	Executes the print process. It is possible to specify the pages to be printed and the number of copies.
Printer Setup	Enables the selection of the required printer and the appropriate port. Some additional options may be specified depending on the particular printer.

Often, special demands are made upon the printout of a worksheet, for example:

- Not the whole worksheet, but only a part of it is to be printed.
- Documentation objectives require the formulas to be printed instead of the calculated values.
- To make the worksheet clearer, the printed worksheet should be allocated a certain fixed text in a header or footer. Page numeration is often desired in the case of large worksheets.
- The worksheet is to be printed with the worksheets co-ordinates, thus with column and row numbers.

We shall deal with the printing procedure and a number of variations by means of the following example:

Exercise 6-1: Printing worksheets

Load the worksheet TURNOVR4.WK4 and specify the following variations for printing:

a) Print the worksheet in Landscape orientation with margins of 1" at the sides. Apply the required settings.

b) Check the settings by means of an example on the screen and save the file as TURNOVR5.WK4.

c) Print the worksheet on the installed printer exactly as shown on the screen.

6.1   Standard settings for printing

1-2-3/W makes use of the printers which you have installed under Windows. Thus initially, the default Windows printer will be used. However, it is possible to deviate from this. Other settings for the printer can also be easily made in the program.

6.1.1   Specifying the printer

Prior to selecting the *Print* command, you must check whether the print settings have been correctly specified. You must be aware of which printer is the default printer.

If you wish to select a different printer, select the *Printer Setup* option from the *File* menu. The corresponding dialog window appears.

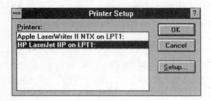

The Printer Setup window

All printers which have been installed under Windows
are now shown in a list. The default printer is highlighted. In our example, that is the HP LaserJet IIP. If
additional printers have been installed, you can select
one of them from the list. Depending on the actual capa-
bilities of the selected printer, you can specify further
options by means of the Setup button in the dialog window. In the case of the HP LaserJet IIP, that dialog box
looks something like this:

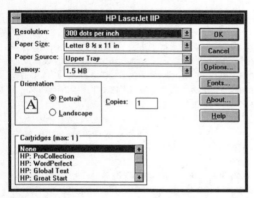

Printer Setup

The options have the following significance:

■ Paper Source determines which tray is to be used
  and how the paper is to be loaded.
■ Paper Size refers to the format of the paper.

■ The Orientation box enables you to select either Portrait or Landscape. The latter option means that the file will be printed horizontally.

If you select the Options button and then the Advanced button, you can make additional specifications:

■ If you wish to make use of a cartridge containing fonts, you must select this from the appropriate list.
■ The Memory box enables you to specify the amount of virtual memory to be used.
■ The Resolution option in the Graphics box determines the number of dots per inch.

Click on OK or press Enter to activate any modifications. You will return to the Options box and then to the Printer Setup dialog window.

Note: You can only use printers which have been installed in Windows if you wish to print under 1-2-3/W. If you wish to use a different printer, you must first configure it in via the Windows Control Panel, Printers.

6.1.2   Specifying the page setup

1-2-3/W provides several methods of defining the layout of a page to be printed. These include:

■ the orientation: Portrait or Landscape
■ the margins
■ headers and footers
■ reproduction options such as borders, column and row titles and numbers
■ sizing the worksheet, ie. scaling it up or down on paper.

Select the *Page Setup* option from the *File* menu. The corresponding dialog box appears:

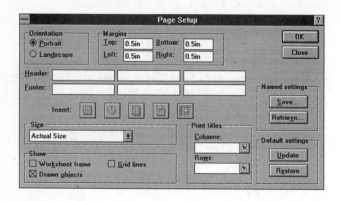

Page Setup window

The options have the following significance:

option	significance
Orientation	Specifies vertical (Portrait) or horizontal (Landscape) page layout.
Margins	Enables you to specify the individual margins, in inches.
Header	Enables you to enter a text to be printed at the top of the page.
Footer	Enables you to enter a text to be printed at the bottom of the page.
Size	Enables you to specify the size of the re-produced text; smaller means you will be able to print more data on the page, larger means that the data will be reproduced larger.
Print titles	Specifies the columns to print as a vertical heading at the left of every page and the rows to print at the top of every page.
Show	Determines whether the worksheet frame, drawn objects and/or grid lines should be printed on the worksheet printout.

The following options are the default settings:

Margins:

Top   This refers to the margin at the top of the paper; this is normally set to 0.5 in.

Left   The left margin is also normally 0.5 in.

Bottom   The margin at the bottom is also normally 0.5 in.

Right   The right margin is also normally 0.5 in.

Headers and footers, grid lines and column letters and row numbers are not normally reproduced unless deliberately specified.

Alterations to the margins are generally made to regulate printing on paper with a logo or company name.

In our example, first alter the margin settings and set the orientation to Landscape. The figure below illustrates the required settings:

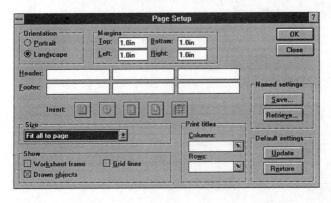

Altered settings in the Page Setup window

When the new settings have been confirmed by pressing Enter, the changes are carried out immediately. Save the result under the name TURNOV50.WK4.

The Page Setup window also contains the Default settings group. If you have made alterations which you later regret, you can restore the old settings by selecting the Restore option here. If you choose Update, the default settings are replaced by the settings which you have just specified.

Note: Print options, once they have been specified, can be saved by assigning a name to these settings. This enables you to activate them as a whole in any other similar applications. To do this, select the Save button in the Named Settings group. In the dialog box which subsequently appears, specify the name of the new group of settings. By activating the Retrieve button in the same group you can bring them into operation later.

6.2   Print Preview

Prior to actually starting printing, it is advisable to display an example of the printout on the screen. The standard display on the screen does not show the worksheet as it will appear on paper; it is only when you use the Print Preview that you can examine changes, to the margins for instance, which are not visible in the normal worksheet.

Select a section of the worksheet which you would like to examine in this way, or specify the appropriate range in the Selected Range text box. Then select the *Print Preview* option from the *File* menu.

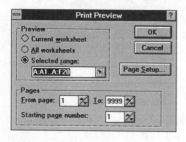

The Print Preview window

The selected range appears in the relevant text box. You can also specify the range now by typing the range or by clicking on the icon and then dragging the cell pointer across the worksheet.

If you now click on OK, an example of the selected range will appear on the screen as it would be printed on the printer under the current settings. A frame indicates the margins.

Pressing Esc returns you to the worksheet. A grey dotted line encloses the specified area.

Note:

■ In the case of several pages, only the first page is initially shown. The first two icons in the top left-hand corner enable you to move to the following page and back to the previous one.

■ The print area may contain any chosen amount of ranges from the currently active worksheet. Define several areas by specifying the ranges, separated from one another by a comma or semi-colon.

■ A print preview will undoubtedly save unnecessary wastage of paper in the long run.

6.3   Layout details when printing

In general, there are severe demands on the quality of worksheet printouts. In order to be able to meet these demands, you should be aware of the following possibilities in the print layout.

Exercise 6-2: Print layout

Open the TURNOV50.WK4 worksheet and execute the following tasks:

a) The worksheet should display the following header:
   -   left-aligned: '1992 Turnover analysis: Fagin Ltd.'

- right-aligned: the page number, for instance Page 2.
b) The footer should contain the following information:
  - left-aligned: the current date, for instance '1/11/93'.
  - right-aligned: the name of the bookkeeper, for instance 'Registered by B.Sikes'.
c) The worksheet is to be printed with row numbers, column letters and grid lines.
d) Check the settings using a print preview on the screen. Save the worksheet under the name TUR-NOV51.WK4.
e) Print the worksheet on the printer.

6.3.1 Printing a worksheet with headers and footers

It is often necessary to provide additional information along with a printout, although the information itself does not actually belong to the worksheet. Accordingly, 1-2-3/W enables you to add headers and footers when printing. This can be very convenient, especially if the worksheet consists of several pages.

For instance, the name of the bookkeeper and the company log or the name of the file could be displayed in the header. In this case, these are texts which can be typed normally.

Variable data can also be shown in a header or footer, for example page numbers in worksheets consisting of several pages. To do this, specify the number sign (#) in the header or footer. This leads to consecutive numbering of the pages.

The header is aligned and printed immediately under the top edge of each page. The following characters can be used to produce special effects:

■ # (the number sign): this produces consecutive page numbering beginning at 1.

- ## (double number sign): defines a different starting number for page numbering. Example: ##4 means that the pages are numbered starting at number 4.
- @ shows the system date on each page in the dd/mm/yy notation.
- \ (backslash): a backslash reproduces data from a cell or range of cells in the header or footer.

The three boxes behind Header and Footer are used to specify left-aligned, centred and right-aligned data respectively.

You are now in a position to execute exercise (a).

6.3.2   Printing the worksheet frame

It is possible to print the worksheet along with the column letters and row numbers. The frame appears on each page.

You can now execute the remaining exercises. The dialog window should eventually appear similar to this:

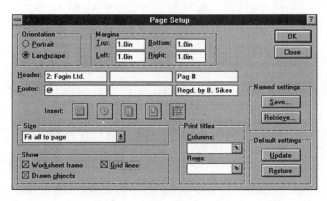

Completed Page Setup dialog window

Check the settings made by means of a print preview on the screen. The headers and footers can be seen here.

(You can activate the magnifying glass+ icon by clicking on it if you wish to have a closer look at your print preview.)

Save the result under the name TURNOV51.WK4.

Note: It is also possible to activate the Grid Lines option (*File, Page Setup, Show*). Normally this option is switched off in 1-2-3/W. It is advisable to leave this option off if you have designed the worksheet layout yourself.

6.3.3   Printing the worksheet along with rows and columns

It is also possible to print the worksheet along with the rows and columns.

Exercise 6-3: Sizing the printouts; printing rows and/or columns

Open the TURNOV51.WK4 worksheet and make the following modifications for the printout:

a) The worksheet is to be printed in Portrait orientation. No borders are to be specified when determining the print area.
b) Column A is to be printed.
c) The worksheet is to be enlarged to 120%.
d) Examine a print preview of the worksheet with altered settings. Force a page break between the third and fourth column.
e) Save the result under the name TURNOV52.WK4.

Particularly in cases of worksheets which have several pages, it is essential to reproduce a certain column or row heading on each page in order to make the information legible. To do this, select the *Page Setup* option from the *File* menu. In the Print Titles box, you can specify which columns are to be printed at the left-hand

side of the paper when several pages are to be printed.
You can also specify the rows which are to be printed
along the top.

When selecting the area to be printed, these rows and
columns must not be marked. Accordingly, first select
the range in the worksheet B1..F20.

Then select the *Page Setup* option from the *File* menu
and specify the following settings:

■ Orientation: Portrait
■ Print Titles: Columns A1..A20.

In this way, the data from column A will be printed on
each page.

6.3.4 Sizing the worksheet printout

As soon as a worksheet no longer fits onto one page, all
kinds of trouble may arise with different page endings.
The options from the Size box make dealing with this
problem quite straightforward. If automatic sizing is applied, the program will determine the sizing factor itself.
In the case of large worksheets, this may be detrimental
to the legibility of the data. It may be better to specify the
sizing factor yourself.

This is done by selecting Manually Scale from the Size
box.

Note: If the worksheet also contains a diagram or chart,
this too will be sized. The link between charts and worksheets is dealt with in chapter 11.

6.3.5 Forcing a page break

If you are not satisfied with the page breaks which are
automatically applied, it is possible to determine these
yourself.

In our exercise, the procedure is as follows:

- Select column D.
- Open the *Style* menu and select the *Page Break* command.
- Activate the column option.
- Click on OK or press Enter.

Examine the modifications using the *Print Preview* option from the *File* menu.

6.4   Options for the final print procedure

Before finally printing the worksheet, it is still possible to specify a number of options, for instance, the number of copies or a selection of the pages to be printed. Printing can only take place if the worksheet range or the entire worksheet has been selected. If this is not already the case, you must first select the required range before proceeding.

Then select the *Print* option from the *File* menu. The following dialog window appears:

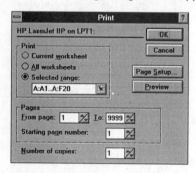

The Print dialog window

The options in this window have the following significance:

option   significance

Print   In addition to the Current Worksheet and
            All Worksheets options, it is possible to
            define one or more ranges for printing.
            The easiest method is to select the range
            first then the *Print* command. In that case,
            the required range is already filled in.

Pages   This group enables you to specify the
            pages to be printed and the number to be
            shown on the first page.

The following buttons are also available in this window:

■ Page Setup in order to activate the window of the
  same name.
■ Preview in order to display a print preview on the
  screen.

When you have concluded all the preliminary work for
printing, you can print the current worksheet immediately. Click on the OK button in the *Print* window to do so. If
everything has gone smoothly, the printed worksheet
should correspond to the specified settings. The pages
are ended according to the specified margins and the
selected font size, or according to the settings specified
using the *Page Break* option from the *Style* menu.

It may occur that the printout does not correspond to the
settings specified. The computer can react in one of two
ways to a print command:

a) An error message may appear on the screen instead
   of the print command being implemented. Possible
   causes are:
   - You have forgotten to connect the printer.
   - The connected printer is not yet configured to the
      program in use.

b) The printout format does not satisfy the expectations. In that case, you must make alterations using the *Page Setup* option from the *File* menu.

Summary of chapter 6

■ Worksheets, diagrams and other data files are printed by means of the *Print* command from the *File* menu. The range to be printed should be defined in advance.

■ General print options are specified using the *Printer Setup* option from the *File* menu: paper source, orientation etc.

■ A worksheet can be printed with headers and footers; worksheets consisting of several pages can be compressed for printing; they can also be allocated title rows and columns on each page. The worksheet frame can also be printed. These options are specified by means of the *Page Setup* option from the *File* menu.

■ The *Print Preview* option from the *File* menu enables you to display an example of the worksheet with the specified settings. This facility is also provided by the *Print* dialog window.

7   Three-dimensional worksheets

The examples in previous chapters dealt with a single worksheet. However, 1-2-3/W also provides the facility of managing no less than 256 worksheets in one collected file. This is referred to as 'three-dimensional spreadsheets'.

The characteristic feature of three-dimensional spreadsheet programs is that they are not restricted to one worksheet window. They manage successive worksheets and make straightforward links between them. Just as the various pages of a voluminous notebook, the individual worksheets of an application are gathered into one file. The result of this is the so-called 3D spreadsheet.

7.1   Advantages of three-dimensional spreadsheets

The concept of three-dimensional worksheets is based on the requirement to edit different worksheets next to each other and, at the same time, bringing them into relation with each other. This occurs by quite simply creating the relationships when constructing the formulas. Instead of addressing only cells in the currently active worksheet, it is possible to address a cell outside this worksheet. Accordingly, each modification in the currently active worksheet can have an effect on the worksheet to which it is related.

The new, third dimension can take on different meanings in practice:

The Time aspect: worksheets containing data from different periods can be linked. The benefits are obvious.

- Different worksheets containing daily figures can be collected into one summary of weekly or monthly information.
- Monthly or quarterly statistics can be bound into one annual report.
- Alterations in turnover figures for last year, for example, in comparison to this year, can be established by placing the corresponding worksheets from last year behind the currently active worksheet.

The Place aspect: Data from different areas are gathered to a central point and reflect a general overview. For instance:

- Worksheets showing turnover, returns and profits from different branches can be adopted into one file to produce a total overview.
- Worksheets containing data about the different marketing areas of a company can be managed in one file; the data are consolidated into one overview.

The Personnel aspect: separate functions and their activities can be reduced to one denominator. For instance, in the context of budgeting, the data from individual departments are initially recorded as separate worksheets and then become one component of the total planning in another worksheet.

Many functions can also be carried out by consolidating the traditional two-dimensional worksheets. However, this is much more laborious and prone to error.

In addition, three-dimensional worksheets provide the following advantages:

- Modifications to a worksheet section are immediately passed on to other linked worksheets.
- Instead of one large, complicated worksheet, there are smaller, more accessible worksheets which are managed in one collected file.

7.2 Constructing 3D worksheets

In general, a two-dimensional worksheet serves as the basis for the construction of three-dimensional worksheets. Because the other worksheets which are managed in the context of a large application are largely similar in structure, it is possible to copy the basic data and formulas to them from the original worksheet. The worksheets which are created in this way can subsequently be equipped with more specialized data. If necessary, it is also possible to consolidate data from the various worksheets to form one file.

Summarizing, the procedure is as follows:

- Create a worksheet which serves as the basis for the other worksheets.
- Ensure that other worksheets are available.
- Copy the first worksheet (basis texts, fixed data and formulas).
- Add specialized data to the appropriate worksheets (texts, values).
- Consolidate the data in a new worksheet.

These steps will be outlined using an example. The TURNOVR4.WK4 worksheet from the previous chapter will be used. This involves the estimated and the real figures of a company branch. We shall assume that the company has four different branches.

In addition to the existing worksheet for the West branch, three similar worksheets should be created for the North, East and South branches. In order to be able to make mutual comparisons, the different worksheets are to be saved in one file. The four worksheets are to be consolidated into one worksheet later to calculate the total company financial situation.

Exercise 7-1: Constructing three-dimensional work-sheets

Open the TURNOVR4.WK4 worksheet and proceed as follows:

a) Insert two empty rows at the top of the worksheet and type 'West branch (financial year 1992)'.
b) Insert three other worksheets behind the currently active worksheet for the other branches.
c) Show the created worksheets in perspective.
d) Copy the first worksheet to the other worksheets.
e) Type the new titles on the first row of the worksheets B to D. Enter the corresponding values in columns B and D.
f) Save the new worksheet under the name TUR-NOV43.

7.3   Inserting worksheets

The first step is to open the TURNOVR4.WK4 file using the *Open* command from the *File* menu. Insert the two empty rows at the top of the worksheet by positioning the cell pointer at A1 and then marking the range A1..A2. Now open the *Edit* menu and select the *Insert* option. Activate the Row button if necessary. Click on OK (or press Enter). Add the new text to the new rows.

Additional worksheets have to be made for the other branches. Again select the *Insert* option from the *Edit* menu. Now select the Sheet option in the subsequent dialog box. You must specify whether the new sheets are to be inserted in front of or after the current work-sheet. We shall select After in our example. Enter the required number in the Quantity box; the maximum is 256; we require 3.

Make the appropriate specifications.

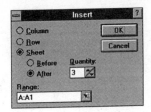

The dialog box for inserting worksheets

When you confirm the specifications by clicking on OK or pressing Enter, the screen will look like this:

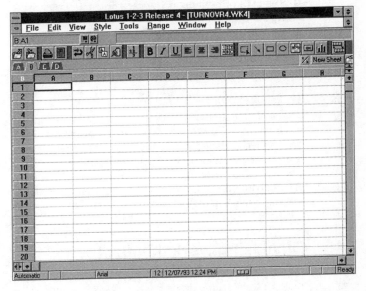

The screen when the worksheets have been inserted

Tip: A quick method of inserting three new worksheets is to click three times on the New Sheet button at the extreme right-hand side of the row containing the worksheet tabs.

You will notice that the second worksheet is active. The worksheet tab is highlighted and the tab letter is shown

in the address area B:A1. This means that the cell
pointer is in cell A1 of worksheet B. The worksheet itself
contains no data as yet. There are four tab letters
shown on the tab line.

The following summary gives an outline of the worksheet insertion procedure:

- Open the *Edit* menu using Alt-E or by clicking on the
  name.
- Activate the *Insert* option by clicking on it or by press-
  ing I.
- Select the Sheet option by clicking on it or by press-
  ing Alt-S.
- Select After by clicking on it or by pressing Alt-F.
- Enter the number of sheets in the Quantity box (press
  Q).
- Execute the command by clicking on OK or pressing
  Enter.

Check if three new, empty worksheets have indeed
been created. To do this, you have to switch between
the opened worksheets. This can be done by pressing
the key combinations Ctrl-PgUp and Ctrl-PgDn. When
you have reached worksheet D, Ctrl-PgUp will not take
you any further. You can also switch between worksheets by clicking on the worksheet tab letters.

7.4   Displaying worksheets in perspective

Up until now, only one worksheet has been shown at
one time, even if several worksheets were opened. In
order to increase the ease of comprehension and to
provide comparisons, it is now possible to display three
worksheets simultaneously on the screen in 1-2-3/W.
To do this, first select worksheet A. Then select the *Split*
option from the *View* menu. In the subsequent dialog
box, select the Perspective option from the Type group.
The screen displays three worksheets.

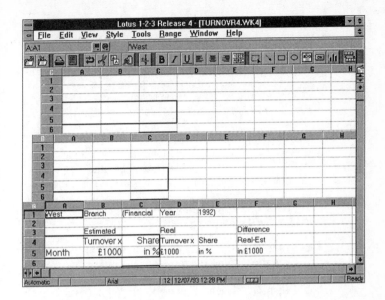

The worksheets in perspective

As you see, worksheet A is active at the bottom of the screen. The worksheets B and C are visible above.

In order to be able to move directly to particular cell addresses in selected worksheets, you will need to use various function keys as well as the mouse.

key (combination)	significance
Ctrl-PgUp	Move to the next worksheet (eg. from B to C).
Ctrl-PgDn	Move to the previous worksheet.
F6	Switches between the worksheets displayed on the screen.
Ctrl-Home	Move the cell pointer to cell A1 of the first worksheet (A:A1).

End, Ctrl-Home | Move the cell pointer to the last worksheet in the file and to the position equivalent to the lowest, rightmost cell containing data in *any* of the worksheets in the file.

End, Ctrl-PgUp | Move to the next worksheet containing data, the same cell position.

End, Ctrl-PgDn | Move to the next worksheet containing data.

F5, cell address, Enter | Go to specified cell address.

Try out these combinations in, for instance, the following activities.

■ Press Ctrl-PgUp. When you have done this twice, worksheet A will disappear from your screen. Worksheet D will take its place.

■ Press Ctrl-PgDn to move to worksheet B and then press Ctrl-Home. The cell pointer moves to cell A1 in worksheet A.

■ Press the GoTo key (F5) and type C:D5 in the Range box. When you press Enter, the cell pointer moves immediately to the proper cell.

Go back to worksheet A and remove the Perspective view. To do this, select the *Clear Split* option from the *View* menu.

7.5   Copying worksheets within a file

In the following stage, the estimated and the real turnover figures from the North, East and South branches are to be adopted into worksheets B to D. Since all four worksheets have the same basic structure, it is advisable to use worksheet A as the basis, in other words to use it as the prototype for the other worksheets. The variable data can be filled in afterwards.

In order to ensure that the settings are valid for all worksheets, you must first activate the GROUP mode. Then all settings in the current basic worksheet can be applied to the others.

In our example, all data in worksheet A are to be copied to worksheets B to D. Place the cell pointer at A1 of the basic worksheet using Ctrl-Home. Now activate the GROUP mode by opening the *Style* menu and selecting the *Worksheet Defaults* option. Place a cross in the GROUP mode box (click on it or press G). When you have clicked on OK or have pressed Enter, the status bar displays the word Group.

Now mark the range you wish to copy. In our example, this is almost the entire visible worksheet (A1..F20). Do this using Shift-Cursor keys or using the mouse. Then select the *Copy* command from the *Edit* menu. Click on tab B or press Ctrl-PgUp. Ensure that the cell pointer is located on B:A1 and select *Edit, Paste*. Then move to worksheet C, cell A1 and select *Edit, Paste* and then go to worksheet D and do the same. Now all worksheets are filled with data from worksheet A. Select *View, Split, Perspective, OK* and the screen will appear as shown on the following page.

The contents of worksheets B to D are identical to those in worksheet A. Proceed as follows to create the required file.

- Alter the titles of worksheets B to D by typing the relevant branch headings.
- Remove the invalid data from columns B and D.
- Type the correct data in columns B and D.

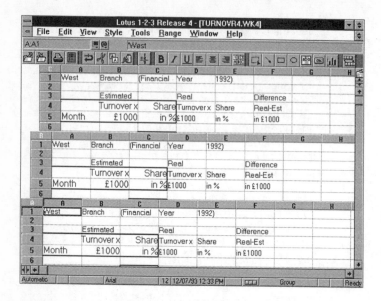

The screen when worksheet A has been copied

Changing the worksheet headings

Position the cell pointer in cell A1 of each worksheet and type:

■ in worksheet B: North Branch Financial Year 1992
■ in worksheet C: East Branch Financial Year 1992
■ in worksheet D: South Branch Financial Year 1992

As you already know, you can activate the Edit mode by pressing F2 and thus easily alter the cell contents.

Changing the column contents

When working with three-dimensional worksheets in the GROUP mode, you can remove the contents of a column in all worksheets in one go. In our case, this will be applied to the estimated turnover figures. To do this, select the *Clear* command from the *Edit* menu. Specify the relevant range in the Range box B:B7..D:B18.

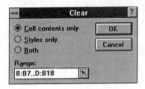

The Clear dialog box

When you have confirmed this using OK or by pressing Enter, the cell contents in the range B7..B18 in the worksheets B to D are removed. The figure below illustrates this:

	A	B	C	D	E	F	G	H
7	january		0.0	132	3.9	132		
8	february		0.0	260	7.6	260		
9	march		0.0	322	9.4	322		
10	april		0.0	312	9.2	312		
11	may		0.0	322	9.4	322		
12	june		0.0	457	13.4	457		
13	july		0.0	234	6.9	234		

	A	B	C	D	E	F	G	H
7	january		0.0	132	3.9	132		
8	february		0.0	260	7.6	260		
9	march		0.0	322	9.4	322		
10	april		0.0	312	9.2	312		
11	may		0.0	322	9.4	322		
12	june		0.0	457	13.4	457		
13	july		0.0	234	6.9	234		

	A	B	C	D	E	F	G	H
7	january	150	4.2	132	3.9	-18		
8	february	212	6.0	260	7.6	48		
9	march	222	6.2	322	9.4	100		
10	april	318	8.9	312	9.2	-6		
11	may	344	9.7	322	9.4	-22		
12	june	551	15.5	457	13.4	-94		
13	july	180	5.1	234	6.9	54		

Three worksheets after the Clear command

Apply the same procedure to column D in worksheets B to D.

Entering the branch data

You can now enter the relevant estimated and real turnover figures for the individual branches in columns B
and D of worksheets B to D.

Note: You may have to adjust the percentage calculation formulas, depending on what you previously entered. Go to cells C7 and E7 of each worksheet and
make sure that the formulas apply to that particular
worksheet. For instance in worksheet C, the formula in
cell C7 should be:

```
+B7*100/C:$B$20
```

If necessary, change the formula by first pressing the
Edit key (F2). Then copy the formula downwards to the
other relevant cells using *Edit, Copy* and *Edit, Paste*.

Now enter the following values:

Month	North Branch (worksheet B) Estimated Turnover	Real Turn-over	East Branch (worksheet C) Estimated Turnover	Real Turn-over	South Branch (worksheet D) Estimated Turnover	Real Turn-over
jan	87	88	192	194	99	88
feb	100	99	201	199	110	122
mar	120	122	200	201	110	129
apr	125	135	210	222	100	115
may	130	144	220	240	120	100
jun	135	140	225	245	125	108
jul	130	128	220	210	122	120
aug	100	101	180	199	110	99
sep	114	120	200	201	114	120
oct	120	134	210	229	125	130
nov	130	143	215	225	122	134
dec	130	133	220	210	130	123

Because all the formulas have already been entered, the statistical data, the percentages and the difference between the estimated and the real turnover are automatically calculated by the program when the new branch data are entered.

The result is as follows when the worksheets B to D are shown in perspective.

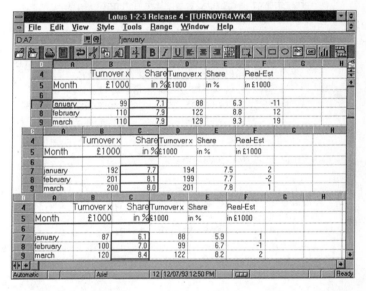

Branch data in perspective

Save the result by selecting *Save* from the *File* menu and assigning the name TURNBRCH.

7.6 Merging worksheets

An important advantage of three-dimensional spreadsheets is the facility of being able to combine different worksheets into one total worksheet. In this way, for instance, the values over various periods or the values for different branches of one company can be combined.

Exercise 7-2: Combining worksheets

Open the TURNBRCH.WK4 worksheet and combine the values from the four worksheets into one worksheet which calculates and displays the total figures for the company. Work through the following stages:

a) Insert a worksheet in front of worksheet A.
b) Show the created worksheets in perspective.
c) Since the new worksheet is to have the same structure as the others, copy worksheet A to the newly-
   made, empty worksheet.
d) In the **new** consolidated worksheet A, enter the title
   'Combined Figures Financial Year 1992'.
e) Have the values in columns B and D added up.
f) Save the new worksheet under the name TURNO-
   TOT.WK4.

Inserting the worksheet

The new worksheet containing the combined data is to be created at the beginning of the file. To do this, position the cell pointer in worksheet A, the worksheet before which a new worksheet is to be inserted. Open the *Edit* menu and select the *Insert* option. Activate the Sheet option in the subsequent dialog box and select Before.

When you have confirmed the command by pressing Enter or clicking on OK, the following result appears on the screen.

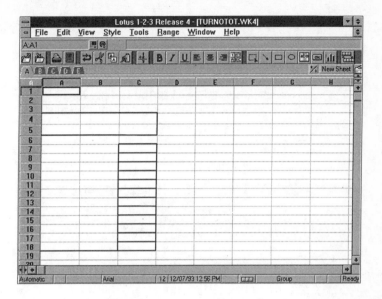

The new Total worksheet

Copying the contents of the worksheet

In order to copy worksheet B to worksheet A, first switch to the Perspective display by means of the *Split* option from the *View* menu. Ensure that the Group mode has been specified (*Style, Worksheet Defaults*). Then mark the data in worksheet B and select the *Copy* command from the *Edit* menu. Then select the new worksheet A and select the *Paste* option from the *Edit* menu. The data from worksheet B are adopted into worksheet A.

Now switch the Group mode off again. Change the title at the top of the worksheet to Combined Figures (Financial Year 1992) and remove the monthly data in columns B and D using the *Clear* option (Cell contents only) from the *Edit* menu.

Specifying the sum

The summed values are to be placed in columns B and D. First activate cell B7 in worksheet A. This cell is to display the sum of the values of the corresponding cells in worksheets B, C, D and E. The formula can be specified by typing the following or by marking the cells:

```
@SUM(B:B7..E:B7)
```

The result is as follows:

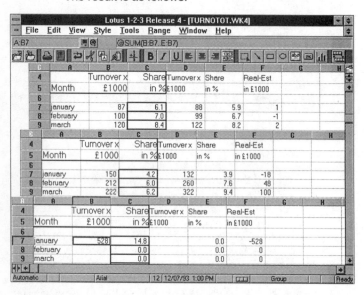

The result of the Sum formula

The result can be copied downwards in column B for the other months. Enter the sum formula in cell D7 of worksheet A in the same way: @SUM(B:D7..E:D7). Copy this formula downwards to the other months in the same column.

Note: Depending on your previous specifications, you may have to change the percentage formulas. Go to cell

C7 in the new worksheet A and make sure that the relevant formula refers to worksheet A. It should be as follows:

```
+B7*100/A:$B$20
```

If necessary, copy the formula downwards using *Edit, Copy* and *Edit, Paste*. Do the same for the formulas in column D.

When you have removed the perspective view (*View, Clear Split*), and have emphasized the title of worksheet A a little, the result will look something like this:

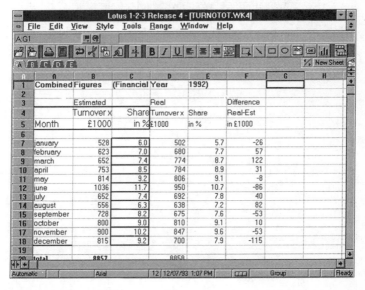

Combined Figures 1992

Summary of chapter 7

- By creating files containing several worksheets, the addressing of corresponding data becomes more simple and quicker. In addition, total calculations and consolidations can be displayed in an orderly manner.
- Three-dimensional worksheets can be efficiently created by adding extra worksheets to a worksheet which has already been created. This is done by selecting the *Insert* option from the *Edit* menu and activating the Sheet option in the subsequent dialog box. The best procedure is then to copy the structure of the worksheet which was first created.
- Various worksheets can be displayed simultaneously in perspective. Select the *Split* option from the *View* menu, then Perspective.
- By combining several worksheets, it is possible to consolidate selected data.

8 Working with windows and linking worksheets

8.1 Application of window techniques

A feature of modern programs is the facility of dividing the screen into various components, thus creating various smaller 'screens' in which work can be done independently of the other sections. This so-called window-technique provides a number of benefits.

In the case of spreadsheets, the advantages can be summarized under three aspects:

Improving the overview in the case of voluminous worksheets. It is possible to display data from different periods adjacent to each other on the screen, making quick comparison very easy. In addition, if the display has been condensed, there is more room to show extra rows and columns on the screen.

Copying becomes easier. By means of the window-technique, it is possible to copy worksheet ranges quite straightforwardly from one worksheet to another.

Comparing in the case of three-dimensional worksheets. It has already been mentioned that three-dimensional worksheets can be displayed in perspective, so that three worksheets are displayed simultaneously on the screen. Comparison is quite simple in cases like these.

The following exercise outlines the possibilities of window-technique in two-dimensional display.

Exercise 8-1: Working with the window-technique

Open the TURNOVR4.WK4 file and try out the possibilities provided by the window-technique using this
example:

a) Display a vertical window.
b) Display a horizontal window.
c) Work within the windows: switch between windows,
examine the zoom function.
d) Condense the display.

8.1.1   Arranging the window settings

Under 1-2-3/W it is possible to split the screen to display
separate windows. To do this, select the *Split* option
from the *View* menu. The following dialog box appears:

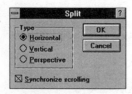

The Split dialog box

The Type group provides three options, only one of
which can be activated at one time. The options have
the following significance:

option	significance
Horizontal	Divides the screen horizontally into two sections, at the row where the cell pointer is currently located.
Vertical	Divides the screen vertically into two sections, the column where the cell pointer is currently located.
Perspective	Three consecutive worksheets can be displayed, overlapping one another (see

chapter 7, *Three-dimensional work-sheets).*

The Synchronize Scrolling option is the default setting and ensures that when you are browsing through the rows and columns in one window, the rows and columns in the other windows move correspondingly. If you do not wish this to happen, you should de-activate this option by clicking on it or move to it using Tab and press the spacebar.

In the file you have just opened, move the cell pointer to column D and select the *Split* command from the *View* menu. Then select the Vertical option. When you confirm your choice by pressing Enter, the screen will be split into two parts and the following appears:

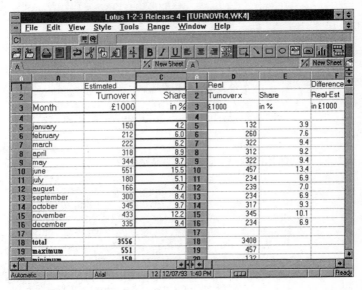

The worksheet after the vertical split

The new window begins at column D. The cell pointer is located in the original window. If you move the cell pointer by pressing Cursor Down or PgDn, you will see

that the rows in the right-hand window move to correspond with those on the left. This is because the Synchronize Scrolling is the default setting. As mentioned,
you can de-activate this by removing the cross in the
relevant box. Try the non-synchronic function to see
which effect this produces. Then activate the option
once more and position the cell pointer on cell A1.

You can split the screen into horizontal windows. Activate the Horizontal option in the *Split* dialog box. The
screen is then divided at the position of the cell pointer.
If the Synchronize Scrolling option is activated, the columns in both windows will move in harmony when you
press the cursor keys.

The screen can also be easily split into horizontal and
vertical windows. To do this, use the split block on the
left of the horizontal scroll bar and at the top of the vertical scroll bar. Click on the split block and drag the line
formed to the required splitting position. The screen is
not split in the same way as in the previous cases; the
window display is reproduced at the position where you
release the line, except for the first line or column. This
makes comparison very easy when the Synchronize
Scrolling option has been de-activated.

8.1.2   Working with separate windows

You can switch back and forward between the windows
using the F6 function key. When switching between the
windows, the computer will react in one of two different
ways, in accordance with the Synchronize Scrolling setting. When the option has been activated, the cell
pointer remains on the same cell when you switch to the
other window. When the option has been de-activated,
you will move to the cell which was previously active in
the new window.

By activating the zoom function using the key combination Alt-F6, it is possible to temporarily alter the size of
the active window. If you press Alt-F6, the active win-

dow is enlarged to its maximum size and occupies the entire screen. Pressing Alt-F6 once again restores the window to its previous size.

It has been mentioned that the windows are able to show sections of the same worksheet and also sections of different worksheets. In the former case, any data entered or commands given apply to both windows; in the latter case, this is not so.

8.1.3 Removing a window

An extra window is removed from the screen as follows:

- Go to the window you wish to remove by pressing F6.
- Open the *View* menu using Alt-V or using the mouse and select the *Clear Split* option.

8.1.4 Zooming in and out

If you wish to have an overview of the layout of a large worksheet, it can be very convenient to make use of a condensed screen display. To do this, select the *Set View Preferences* option from the *View* menu. The dialog window appears as shown below.

The Set View Preferences box

You can gain a condensed view by specifying the value
30, for instance, in the Custom Zoom % box. Try this out
with the TURNOVR4.WK4 worksheet. The result of this
is shown below:

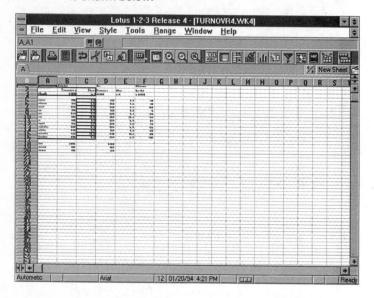

Condensed version on the screen

> *Note:* The Custom Zoom box has a maximum value or
> 400 and a minimum value of 25.

Return to the previous settings.

8.2 Combining worksheets

In a good spreadsheet program, it should be possible to
link worksheets to one another. This expedites the work
considerably and increases the accuracy of the results.

There are various reasons for using results from other
worksheets. One reason is that these results do not
need to be entered, they can be adopted automatically.

The following exercise will illustrate how to adopt data from one worksheet for further editing in another worksheet.

Exercise 8-2: Integrating worksheets

In the following worksheet, there are data which are to be adopted by another worksheet to be further edited. Save this worksheet under the name COSTS1.WK4.

Product cost analysis as specified by the Consumer Goods Department

	Product nr 0899	Product nr 459	Product nr 76	Product nr 86
Development costs	400.00	176.00	450.00	450.00
Material costs	350.00	375.00	250.00	250.00
Manufacturing costs				
overheads	2000.00	1700.00	1700.00	1700.00
var. costs	1100.00	1650.00	1100.00	1100.00
Other costs	900.00	1350.00	900.00	900.00
Total costs	4750.00	5251.00	4400.00	4400.00

Then create the following worksheet and save it under the file name COSTEFF1.WK4.

	Product nr 0899	Product nr 459	Product nr 76	Product nr 86
Sales (quantity)	500	750	500	500
Price p/unit	12.00	12.00	12.00	12.00
Total returns	6000.00	9000.00	6000.00	6000.00
Total costs	4750.00	5251.00	4400.00	4400.00
Net profit	1250.00	3749.00	1600.00	1600.00
Productivity of the investment (in %)	26.3	71.4	36.4	36.4

Now remove the values for the total costs. These values should then be imported from the above worksheet COSTS1.WK4.

We shall now create the first worksheet. This will serve as source worksheet. The total costs which are calculated here are to be used in other worksheets. To make this possible, the range containing the results must be given a name, for example, TOT_COSTS. Go with the cell pointer to field B13 and select the *Name* option from the *Range* menu. Specify the name TOT_COSTS in the subsequent Name box. Specify the range B13..E13 in the Range box. Then save the worksheet under the name COSTS1.

Subsequently, create the worksheet COSTEFF1.WK4 and delete the data from the row containing the total costs. Combining the worksheets takes place via the *Open* command from the *File* menu. Using this, an entire worksheet or a part of it can be transported to the currently active worksheet. The entry then takes place at the current position of the cell pointer. For this reason, it is useful to place the cell pointer at the required position (here B8) before you activate the command. Select the *Open* command from the *File* menu, the COSTS1.WK4 file from the list of files and the Combine button in the dialog box. The screen will appear as follows:

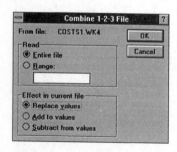

Combine 1-2-3 File box

The figure shows that there are three options in the menu to combine data from another file with the current worksheet:

Replace values	Copies the contents of the cells to the current worksheet.
Add to values	Adds the values of the cell contents to the values in the current worksheet. This can be useful, for instance, if various monthly worksheets have to be added to a quarterly or annual worksheet.
Subtract from values	Subtracts the cell contents from the values in the cells in the current worksheet.

For our example, select the Replace Values option. The Read group gives the choice of adopting an Entire File or merely a Range. Select the second option, since we only wish to copy a part and not the entire file. A name has to be specified for this range, TOT_COSTS in this case.

When the command has been confirmed, the selected data should be automatically copied to row 8 of the current worksheet. In this way, updating can be easily implemented if alterations take place in the source worksheet.

Keep the following points in mind:

■ The allocation of range names makes it more easy to adopt certain worksheet ranges. Otherwise, you must specify the exact cell addresses of the range to be adopted.
■ When adopting data from other files, the notation remains the same. Thus, alterations to the layout and notation may be necessary.

Summary of chapter 8

■ By dividing the screen into horizontal or vertical windows, it is possible to increase the overview of voluminous worksheets and to simplify certain tasks.

■ The window key F6 enables you to switch between the different windows which have been created using the *Split* option from the *View* menu.

■ The Combine button from the *Open* command in the *File* menu enables you to combine various worksheets. The options provided in the combining process are Replacing, Adding or Subtracting the values of the source worksheet when importing data to the active worksheet.

■ The following list shows all the options available when combining worksheets:

Replace values	Copies the cell contents to the active worksheet.
Add to values	Add the values of the cell contents to the values already in the active worksheet. This may be convenient if, for instance, different monthly worksheets have to be summed up to form a quarterly or annual report.
Subtract from values	Subtracts the values of the cell contents from those in the currently active worksheet.

9 Special functions in worksheet calculations

1-2-3/W provides a large amount of functions which help simplify working with the program. We have already dealt with a number of statistical functions such as the calculation of sums and minimum and maximum values. In principle, functions in 1-2-3/W are applied as follows:

- Activate the cell in which the function is to be placed;
- Type the at sign (@);
- Type the required function with the appropriate parameters.

It is possible to select the required function from a list. It is then adopted into the Contents box. In this case too, you should first activate the cell in which the function is to be located. Then type the at sign. If you now press F3, the following dialog box will appear containing a list of all applicable functions.

List of @ functions

Select the required function from this list and then click on OK. The function is shown in the Contents box. You can also click on the icon for the @ functions in the Edit line. A list of the commonly-used functions will be displayed from which you can select one directly. If the function you wish to use is not shown here, select the *List All* option. A window appears, identical to that shown in the figure.

Use the method you prefer.

We shall deal extensively with a number of functions using examples as points of reference:

■ logical functions: simple logical claims, logical connections and multiple choices
■ the capital value function and functions to calculate the depreciation values, being examples of functions for application of financial mathematical functions
■ time and date functions.

9.1   Logical functions in practice

Many aspects of business life are determined by decisions based on variable data. In this area, the spreadsheet can work through various scenarios by means of logical functions, making complex applications more accessible.

9.1.1   Simple logical applications

Using the following exercise, we shall describe the application of logical functions.

Exercise 9-1: Sales commission

The following worksheet must calculate the commission of the salesmen in a company. A commission of 5% of the annual turnover is available if the turnover is greater than £400,000. Otherwise a fixed sum of £10,000 will be paid. Unfortunately, not all the salesmen will strike it rich.

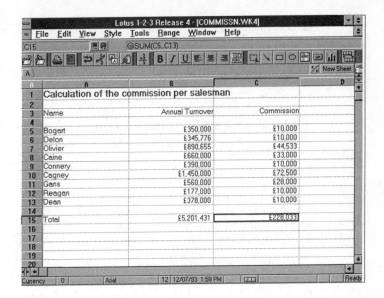

The final commission worksheet

Notes:
- The width of all columns should be 20.
- The worksheet should be saved under the name COMMISSN.WK4.

The aim of this worksheet is to calculate the commission sum. In order to do this, the worksheet should be constructed in the following stages:

- The column width should be set to the standard width of 20 characters by specifying the number 20 in the *Worksheet Defaults* window from the *Style* menu. Enter the number in the Column Width box.
- Enter the title in the first row using a larger font. This is done using the *Font & Attributes* option from the *Style* menu.
- Enter text in column A. The headings in cells B3 and C3 are right-aligned by typing inverted commas before the text.

■ Currency values are entered in columns B and D. Specify this via *Styles, Number Format*. Select Currency from the Format box.
■ Enter the sum formula in cell B15:

```
@SUM(B5..B13)
```

In the calculation of the commission, we must make use of the IF function. The syntax of this function is:

```
@IF(condition;x;y)
```

(*Note:* you should use the semi-colon as the argument separator. This is always valid. A comma or point can also be used but you may have to specify this first via the options *Tools, User Setup, International, Punctuation*.)

The condition is examined during calculation of the cell in question. If the condition is seen to be TRUE, then the result is x; otherwise it is y. In the example the condition is B5>400000. If this condition is satisfied, then the calculation is x:B5*0.05. Otherwise it is y:10000.

Thus, the formula in C5 should be:

```
@IF(B5>400000;B5*0.05;10000)
```

When you have entered all this, the screen on the following page will appear:

The formula in C5 can be copied to the cells C6 to C13 using the *Copy* command from the *Edit* menu. Then the sum of the cells C5 to C13 should be entered in C15. The result should produce the desired worksheet. The worksheet should be saved under the name COMMISSN using the *Save* option from the *File* menu.

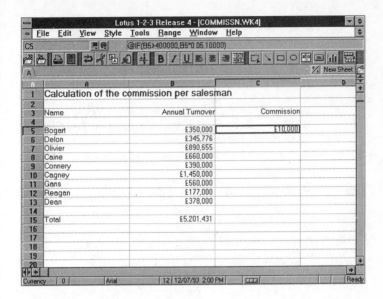

Application of a logical function

9.1.2 Complex functions

Logical functions can also be linked to each other, so that multiple claims are possible. The general syntax is:

```
@IF(condition;x;@IF(condition;x;y))
```

This formula can be extended at will. Keep in mind when constructing a formula like this, that the number of opening brackets must coincide with the number of closing brackets.

We shall apply this in practice in the following example.

Exercise 9-2: Break-even analysis

In this example, we shall make a break-even analysis. The calculation of the profit threshhold is an important aid when deciding whether or not your proposed new product should actually be brought into production. The worksheet which we shall create provides a model for this application. The following steps are to be implemented:

■ First enter the data under the information section.
■ Then specify the formulas in a way that they can easily be copied downwards.
■ Save the file under the name BREAK.

Break-even analysis: calculation of the profit threshhold

Data:

Returns per article	360		
Var. cost/article	152		
Abs. fixed costs	50000		
Var. fixed costs	30000	initial amount	850
Amount interval	500	analysis interval	25

Calculation and analysis

Amount	Returns	Var. costs	Abs. fixed costs	Var. fixed costs	Total costs	Profit
850	306000	129200	50000	60000	239200	66800
875	315000	133000	50000	60000	243000	72000
900	324000	136800	50000	60000	246800	77200
925	333000	140600	50000	60000	250600	82400
950	342000	144400	50000	60000	254400	87600
975	351000	148200	50000	60000	258200	92800
1000	360000	152000	50000	90000	292000	68000
1025	369000	155800	50000	90000	295800	73200
1050	378000	159600	50000	90000	299600	78400
1075	387000	163400	50000	90000	303400	83600
1100	396000	167200	50000	90000	307200	88800
1125	405000	171000	50000	90000	311000	94000
1150	414000	174800	50000	90000	314800	99200
1175	423000	178600	50000	90000	318600	104400
1200	432000	182400	50000	90000	322400	109600
1225	441000	186200	50000	90000	326200	114800
1250	450000	190000	50000	90000	330000	120000
1275	459000	193800	50000	90000	333800	125200
1300	468000	197600	50000	90000	337600	130400

In the example, there are seven separate fields for data in the upper part. With regard to these fields, calculations are made in the lower part. Here, taking a random amount, an analysis of any situation can be made.

The formulas in the lower part must be constructed in such a way that they can be applied to the rows below using the *Copy* command. In the columns of the first row (row 17), we find the following construction of the diverse formulas:

(1) Calculation of the amount (column 1): as the initial amount, the number in cell F8 is adopted in A17, and then the following formula is applied to cell A18: previous cell + analysis interval. In addition, the addressing of cell A17 must be relative, while the reference to the value of the analysis interval must be absolute. For cell A18, this means:

```
A17+$F$9
```

Subsequently, the other cells receive this formula via *Copy* and then *Paste* from the *Edit* menu.

(2) Calculation of the returns (column B): the returns are calculated by multiplying the amount of articles by the returns per article. Here, the field dealing with the quantity should be addressed relatively and the field for the returns per article absolutely. For example:

```
A17*$C$5
```

(3) Variable costs (column C): the variable costs are calculated by multiplying the quantity by the variable costs per article. For example:

```
A17*$C$6
```

(4) Absolute overhead costs (column D): are adopted from field C7. Subsequently, copy downwards.

(5) Variable overheads (column E): in order to calculate the variable overheads, it is necessary to request the appropriate quantity interval. Using the @IF function, a multiple of the staggered sums corresponding to the quantity interval can be calculated. In general, that should take place as follows:

```
@IF(amount<quant.interval;var.overheads;
@IF(amount<quant.interval*2;var.overheads *2;
@IF(amount<quant.interval*3;var.overheads*3;
var.overheads*4)))
```

In our tangible example, that means the following for cell E17:

```
@IF(A17<$C$9;$C$8;@IF(A17<$C$9*2;$C$8*2;
@IF(A17<$C$9*3;$C$8*3;$C$8*4)))
```

(6) Total costs: these are calculated by adding up all the previous costs.

(7) Profit: the profit is the difference between the returns and the total costs.

The benefits of this model lie in the flexible application possibilities. Thus, with variations in the data entered, alternative calculations can be carried out.

9.1.3   A list of logical functions

As the examples show, the application area of 1-2-3/W can be extended by using logical functions. There are a number of important logical functions, which can also be used in combination with each other.

function	significance
@IF(condition;x;y)	if the condition is true, *x* is valid, otherwise *y*.
@ERR	produces the logical value ERR (value 0).
@ISERR(A)	if the argument in question, A, is an ERR value, ISERR returns 1 (true).
@ISNA(A)	tests the argument A for the value NA (Not Available); if this is so the function returns the value 1 (true).
@ISNUMBER(A)	returns the true value (1) if the argument has a numeric value.
@ISSTRING(A)	If argument A is a string, this will return the logical value 1 (true).

9.2 Financial mathematical functions in practice

Spreadsheets provide a great number of functions which simplify financial and investment planning, especially in financial mathematical applications.

We shall deal with these functions in the light of two examples, one with a capital value function and one for the calculation of depreciation figures.

9.2.1 Investment analysis using the capital value function

Exercise 9-3: Applying the capital value function

The following worksheet must calculate the profitability of an investment, based on the capital value method. The returns during the service life are placed opposite the total amount which is to be invested.

The layout of the worksheet is to be as follows:

- The total invested amount is placed in row 3.
- Row 4 contains the estimated service life in years. This is reckoned to be 10 years.
- The expected interest percentage in placed in row 5.
- The estimated returns (income) during the service life are entered in rows 8 to 17 inclusive. In the example, the income is estimated at £15,000 in the first year with an annual increase of 15%.
- The calculated capital value is placed in row 19.
- Finally, row 20 should show, by means of comparison of capital value and total investment, whether the investment is recommended.

Save the worksheet under the name CAPVALUE.WK4.

A value which is only achieved after several years has little significance today. The current value is called capital value in accounting jargon. Calculating the capital value is called discounting; in this procedure an estimated interest percentage is taken into consideration. Accordingly, the forecast for the annual return is:

```
capital value = annual return/interest factor
```

The interest factor is calculated using the formula:

$$(1 + p/100)^n$$

Here, *p* is the interest percentage and *n* is the number of years.

For the calculation of the capital value of annual returns over several years, 1-2-3/W provides a function (Net Present Value) which has the following syntax:

```
@NPV(interest;cash flow range)
```

Using this function, the capital value of the future returns resulting from a capital investment can be calculated. In this, the *interest* is taken to be a fixed percentage, while the concept *cash flow range* represents the range of estimated returns from the investment.

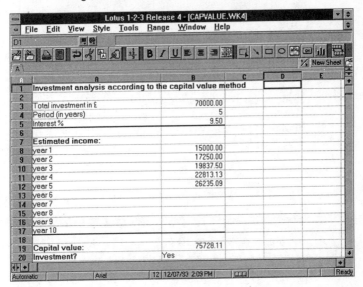

The example worksheet

To carry out the exercise, we shall proceed as follows:

Structure of the worksheet
For the first column, the width should be increased to thiry characters using the *Column Width* option from the *Style* menu. Type 30 in the Set Width To box. Click on OK or press Enter. The second column should have a width of fifteen characters. Then enter the title of the worksheet and the other data.

Formulas to calculate the returns
First, in cell B8, the estimated returns of £15,000 for the first year should be entered. The returns have to be calculated separately in the cells B9..B12. The formula for this is as follows:

```
+B8*1.15
```

Due to the relative reference, it is possible to enter the
formula in B9 alone and then to copy it to cells B10..B12.

Assigning the worksheet range a name

The range containing the returns values should receive
a name. Select the range B8..B17 and then select the
Name option from the *Range* menu. Specify the name
'Returns' in the text box and select Add and then Close.

Calculation of the capital value

The capital value is to be entered in cell B19. We shall
make use of the financial mathematical function which
has the formula:

```
@NPV(B5/100;RETURNS)
```

The screen should appear as follows:

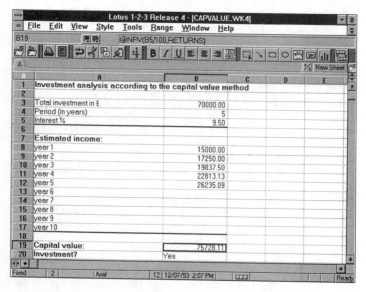

Decision to invest

Finally, in cell B20, the conclusion whether or not to in-
vest should be calculated. The formula is as follows:

```
@IF(B19>B3;"Yes";"No")
```

In the formula, the text data 'Yes' and 'No' are registered as the result possibilities. Remember that when specifying the formula, text must be placed between inverted commas. When the instruction has been implemented, the required worksheet will appear. Save it under the name CAPVALUE.WK4.

9.2.2 Calculation of depreciation

Exercise 9-4: Depreciation worksheet

Different depreciation methods are to be displayed in a comparable survey. In this example, we shall begin with the following values:

- purchase price: £420,000
- service life: eight years
- residual (salvage) value: £20,000

This should produce the worksheet displayed below:

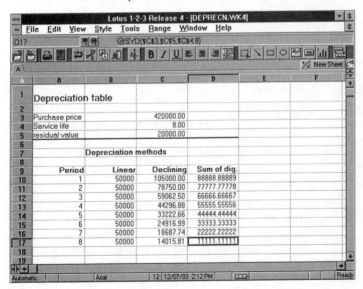

Period	Linear	Declining	Sum of dig.
1	50000	105000.00	88888.88889
2	50000	78750.00	77777.77778
3	50000	59062.50	66666.66667
4	50000	44296.88	55555.55556
5	50000	33222.66	44444.44444
6	50000	24916.99	33333.33333
7	50000	18687.74	22222.22222
8	50000	14015.81	11111.11111

In this example, the global column width should be 12 characters (*Style, Worksheet Defaults*) and the height of row 1 is to be 30 (*Style, Row Height*). Adjust the font in row 1 to 14 points and boldface (*Style, Fonts & Attributes*).
Save the worksheet under the name DEPRECN.WK4.

The 1-2-3/W financial mathematical functions are also used in this example. This concerns:

■ the function to calculate the linear (Straight-Line) depreciation:

```
@SLN(cost;salvage;life)
```

■ to calculate retrogressive (Declining Balance) depreciation:

```
@DDB(cost;salvage;life;period)
```

■ to calculate the sum-of-the-years'-digits depreciation:

```
@SYD(cost;salvage;life;period)
```

First create the basic worksheet. Adjust the layout to the suggested settings. Then enter the known data and values. This will produce the worksheet shown on the following page.

The formula for linear depreciation can now be constructed. First activate cell B10. The formula which is to be entered is as follows:

```
@SLN($C$3;$C$5;$C$4)
```

In this case, all values should be addressed absolutely. Because the values in each year are identical when dealing with linear depreciation, the formula in B10 can be directly copied down to cells B11..B17 using the *Copy* and *Paste* commands from the *Edit* menu. This will produce the worksheet shown on the following page.

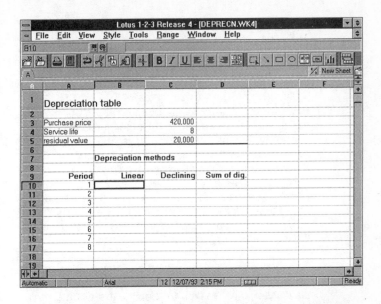

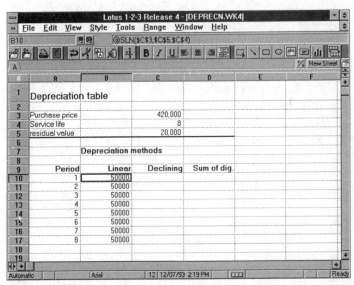

Now the formula for retrogressive (declining balance) depreciation can be placed in C10. The formula is as follows:

```
@DDB($C$3;$C$5;$C$4;1)
```

In the case of retrogressive depreciation, the formula cannot be directly copied to the other cells because the period repeatedly changes. Nevertheless, it is still possible to use the *Copy* and *Paste* instructions. Copy the formula in B10 to all the cells below. Then move to each cell individually and press the Edit key (F2). The corresponding period in each cell should be altered, because the period is different in each case. Thus for period 2, the last number in the formula is 2, for period 3, the last number is 3 etc.

This should produce the worksheet shown below. In addition, you must format the entire range in the Fixed display style with two figures behind the decimal point (*Style, Number Format, Fixed, decimal places 2*).

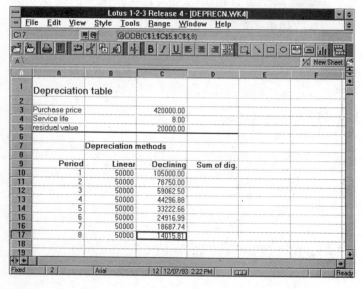

Digital depreciation is calculated in the same way as retrogressive depreciation. Enter the following formula in the cell D10:

```
@SYD($C$3;$C$5;$C$4;1)
```

After copying the formula and correcting the periods, the required worksheet should be complete. Finally, save the worksheet under the name DEPRECN.

9.3 Date and time functions in practice

1-2-3/W supplies not only information about the date and time, it also has functions dealing with these. Useful applications of date and time functions in practice are:

- ■ effective control of payment periods
- ■ calculation of interest to an accuracy of one day
- ■ calculation of time-based wages.

9.3.1 Specifying Date and Time

In order to be able to work with the date and time functions, you must be familiar with the method of specifying and editing date and time data. Attention should be given to several formal rules.

It is possible to specify a date as a text or as a value. If it is to be used in calculations, the date should be entered as a value. The date can, for example, be entered in a cell in the following way: DD:MM:YY. Go to any cell in the worksheet, for instance, A1. Specify the date 05/11/93. The date is automatically right-aligned.

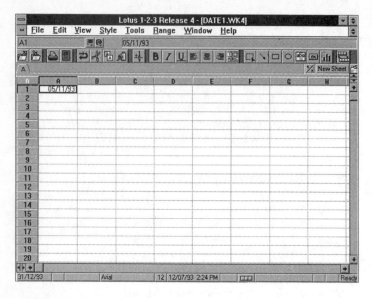

Specifying a date

> When a date is entered, 1-2-3/W recognizes the input
> as being a date and adjusts it. The cell receives the
> Date layout. The date layout in this cell can be altered
> by means of the *Number Format* option from the *Style*
> menu. The corresponding dialog box provides the fol-
> lowing options.

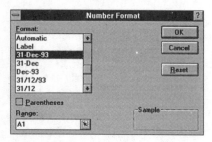

Date options

> Press Enter or click on OK to confirm the alteration.

9.3.2   Calculation using date and time

It is also possible to display the current time. The function @NOW performs this. This function displays the serial number for the current date and time in the active cell.

Try this function out in cell A1. When you have entered @NOW and have confirmed this using Enter, the serial number for the current date and time appears on the screen. If no battery powered clock is integrated in your computer, it is necessary to enter the correct date and time yourself when starting up the computer otherwise this function will not be correctly applied. In 1-2-3/W, dates are displayed as serial integers between 1 and 73,050. 1 corresponds to January 1st 1900, 73,050 corresponds to 31st December 2099.

Using the following exercise, we shall deal with further possibilities for the date and time functions.

Exercise 9-5: Reminders

In order to check whether outstanding debts are paid on time, we shall create a worksheet which :

■ calculates the due date from the invoice date and the fulfilment period;
■ referring to the current date, shows whether a reminder should be sent because the fulfilment period has elapsed.

A list of dubious debtors is to be created.

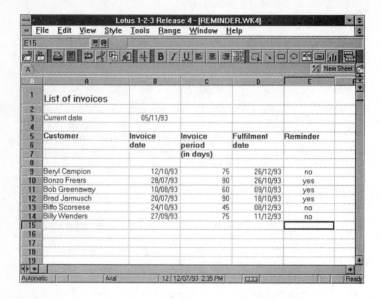

List of invoices

Procedure:

- First enter the text data.
- Then the independent values can be entered in column C (Fulfilment period).
- Then enter the current date in B3 and the invoice dates in B9..B14.
- Format the invoice dates in the desired display.
- Calculate the due dates in column D.
- A text must be entered in column E (Yes or No). This determines whether a reminder should be sent or not.
- Save the worksheet under the name REMINDER.

We shall now apply the input and the format of date specification. Subsequently, we shall examine how this information can be used in calculations.

The solution to the problem can be divided into a number of steps.

a) All text data must be entered at the appropriate positions: the title of the survey and the columns and the names of the customers.

b) The number values must be entered in column C. This deals with the fulfilment period in days.

c) The date input is entered: the current date and also the invoice dates. We shall enter the date (05/11/93) ourselves for reasons of clarity and uniformity, at this moment. In practice however, the @NOW function is probably preferable in order to apply the current date each time the worksheet is activated.

d) Select the *Number Format* option from the *Style* menu to allocate the invoice dates in column B the desired format. Select the option in the form 31/12/93. (If this option is not displayed in your settings go to the *Tools* menu and choose *User Setup*. Select the International button and the Date pulldown menu in the subsequent dialog box. Highlight the required format and press Enter or click on OK twice. The program now recognizes this format.)

e) As mentioned, 1-2-3/W saves the date and time internally as decimal numbers. This enables the execution of mathematical operations using date and time fields, or use of date or time in a formula. In order to calculate the appropriate due dates for the individual invoices, you must add the corresponding fulfilment period to the invoice date. Accordingly, the following formula is created for field D9, which can then be copied downwards:

`+B9+C9`

When the result cells have been formatted in the proper way (*Style, Number Format, Format, 31/12/93 if necessary*), the due date will be accurately shown in column D.

f) Whether or not a reminder should be sent, is determined by comparing the calculated due date to the current date as specified in cell B3. The @IF function will provide the answer.

Thus, in field E9 the following formula should be entered:

```
@IF(D9<$B$3;"Yes";"No")
```

And this formula can also be copied downwards.
Save this worksheet under the name REMINDER using the *Save* command from the *File* menu.

9.4   Exercises

Exercise 1: Calculating an invoice sum

Create the following worksheet using formulas based on fixed data concerning 'Quantity' and 'Price p/unit'. These enable you to calculate the gross sum. If more than 100 articles are ordered a discount of 15% is given.

Calculation of invoice sum			
Data:			
Quantity	98	154	100
Price per unit	25.00	25.00	25.00
Value	2450.00	3850.00	2500.00
Discount	0.00	577.50	0.00
Total net	2450.00	3272.50	2500.00
VAT 17.5%	428.75	572.6	437.5
Invoice sum	2878.75	3845.1	2937.5

Save the worksheet under the name INVOICE.

Exercise 2: Quotation comparison

A spreadsheet can provide valuable assistance when comparing quotations. We shall create a worksheet to calculate various factors.

Quotation comparison for a maximum of three suppliers

Name supplier	Ellington	Hendrix	Monk
Quot.cost price	4500.00	4000.00	4200.00
Discount (in %)	25	30	20
Act.cost price	3375.00	2800.00	3360.00
Credit limit (%)	2	3	5
Net cost price	3307.50	2716.00	3192.00
Supply costs	420.00	350.00	320.00
Total cost price	3727.50	3066.00	3512.00
Most advantageous cost price:	3066.00		

The known values to be entered are:

- the official cost price
- the conditions, such as the quantity discount and credit limits
- the supply costs.

Save the worksheet under the name QUOTATN.

Procedures

For exercise 1:

When the known text and number data are known, calculate the value of the goods in cell B7. Use the formula:

```
+B4*B5
```

This formula can subsequently be copied to cells C7..D7.

The calculation of the discount depends upon the quantity supplied, that is, upon whether this figure is greater than 100. This gives rise to the following formula:

```
@IF(B4>100;B7*0.15;0)
```

Copy this formula twice to the right.

The following formulas apply to the other cells to which they can also be copied:

```
B10:  +B7-B8
B11:  +B10*0.175
B13:  +B10+B11
```

For exercise 2:

When all the known data have been entered, the formulas can be constructed. In order to calculate the actual cost price in row 9, we can use the following formula:

```
quot.cost price - (discount perc. * cost
price / 100)
```

This is:

```
B6-(B7*B6/100)
```

This formula can be adopted in columns C and D using the *Copy* and *Paste* commands from the *Edit* menu. The same applies to the formula which calculates the net cost price.

The cost price is calculated by adding the supply costs (e.g. transport) to the net cost price.

Using a statistical function, the lowest cost price can be determined. Use the @MIN(range) function for this. The range is B15..D15 in this case.

Summary of chapter 9

- Using logical functions it is possible to create complex applications in 1-2-3/W. The @IF function in particular has special significance. This can also be used in conjunction with other functions and makes it possible to apply multiple claim hypotheses.
- The financial mathematical functions in 1-2-3/W provide extensive calculation possibilities for various applications in financial and economic areas.
- Using date and time functions, worksheets can be made for debit and credit administration.

10   Working with macros

It frequently occurs that certain procedures in a worksheet have to repeated a number of times. In order to
avoid having to go through the same manoeuvres time
and again, 1-2-3/W provides the facility of defining macros.

A macro contains commands and other keystrokes
necessary to execute a required task. The macro itself
is included in the worksheet and is allocated a key combination or range name. By activating the key combination it is then possible to execute a certain standard job
quickly and easily.

It is also possible to save a macro in a separate file, a
so-called *macro library*. In that case, it is not only available to the current worksheet but also to all worksheets.

10.1   Macro application

We shall discuss the usage of macros below, using the
basic functions as the point of departure. We wish, however, to emphasize that macros can also be applied in
complex situations. For example:

Interactive macros
It is possible to program a dialogue with the user by em-
ploying the question mark (?) when writing a program.
The execution of the macro is interrupted to allow the
user the opportunity to move the cell pointer or to enter
data.

Self-starting macros (auto-exec macros)
Each time a worksheet is loaded, 1-2-3/W checks
whether there is a macro present which should be automatically started up. This could be, for instance, an ad-
vice macro for writing reminders.

Macros with menus

It is possible to define commands in macros and, in this way, compose your own menus. In this way, users who are not yet fully familiar with the program can be guided through an application.

Extensive discussion about advanced macro commands lies outside the scope of this book. For more information consult the manual and the Help screens.

10.2 Compiling a simple macro

In principle, a macro is constructed in three stages.

- conceptualizing and entering
- assigning a name
- activating.

These stages will be described one by one with reference to the following exercise.

Exercise 10-1: A simple macro

The transport of calculated costs from one worksheet to another can be done automatically by means of a macro if this concerns a frequently recurring procedure. We shall use the COSTEFF1.WK4 worksheet which is to receive information from the COSTS1.WK4 worksheet.

a) Write a macro for this in a suitable range of the COSTEFF1 worksheet.
b) Assign the shortcut key combination \T or the name 'Total Costs' to this macro.
c) Subsequently save the worksheet COSTEFF1 under the name COSTEFF2 and use the macro.

10.2.1   Conceptualizing and entering the macro

When it is clear for which activity a macro is required, a plan of action has to be made. It is advisable to first test all the keystrokes to observe their effects and to note these carefully. In this example, you can make use of the step-by-step procedure as used in exercise 8-2 in chapter 8.

When entering and compiling a macro, a distinction is made between the following variants:

a) Including menu commands

The macro names for menu commands have the same name as the menu command. Accordingly, if you wish to include the command to open a file, include the command {FILE-OPEN}.

b) Adopting data which is to be entered

There are no special rules when adopting data such as file names, range names or texts which are to be displayed. It is however important to specify a prefix in front of a text if this is to be aligned in the worksheet in a particular way.

c) Including function keys

It is also important to know how special keys and function keys should be adopted. In general, they should be specified between braces {}, with the exception of the Enter key. The list of macro keys on the following page shows the required keys and their corresponding significance for constructing a macro.

macro key	significance
~	Enter
{DOWN} or {D}	cursor downwards
{UP} or {U}	cursor upwards
{LEFT} or {L}	cursor leftwards
{RIGHT} or {R}	cursor rightwards
{HOME}	Home
{END}	End
{PGUP}	PgUp
{PGDN}	PgDn
{HELP}	HELP (F1)
{EDIT}	EDIT (F2)
{NAME}	NAME (F3)
{ABS}	ABS (F4)
{GOTO}	GOTO (F5)
{PANE}	PANE (F6)
{QUERY}	QUERY (F7)
{TABLE}	TABLE (F8)
{CALC}	CALC (F9)
{ALT},{MB},{MENUBAR}	MENU (F10)
{ESCAPE} or {ESC}	Esc
{BACKSPACE} or {BS}	Backspace
{DELETE} or {DEL}	Del
{INSERT} or {INS}	Ins

Notes:

■ The names of the macro keys can be entered using both small and capital letters.
■ The tilde ~ can be obtained by pressing the corresponding key on the keyboard. If it is not available, press Alt-126 (numbers from the numeric keypad, right).

A complete list of macros will be shown when you type a brace { and then press F3. If you wish to gain further information about the macro, select the macro from this list and press F1 or click on the ? in the top right-hand corner of the Macro Keywords dialog box.

The macro in our example is as follows:

```
{GOTO}B8~{FILE-COMBINE
"replace";"COSTS1.WK4";;"TOT_COSTS"}
```

Note: If you saved the COSTS1.WK4 file on diskette in drive A:, you will have to specify this in the command, thus: "A:\COSTS1.WK4".

The example illustrates that a macro may contain both special macro keys (between braces) and normal characters from the keyboard.

Now load the worksheet COSTEFF1. First, remove the range B8..E8 from the worksheet. To construct the macro, an empty range must be found to prevent data which may be present influencing the macro. Go to cell B20 for example.

Now enter the above macro. The macro should be entered in the form of a label. Accordingly, an alignment character (an apostrophe) should be placed if the macro begins with a command, a number or a formula. The screen should appear as shown on the following page.

When entering a macro, the following formal rules should be kept in mind:

■ The macro should be placed in one particular column. In order to be sure that the macro will not be damaged by the insertion or removal of rows, it is advisable to record the macro at the bottom right-hand side of a worksheet.
■ A macro command may contain a maximum of 512 characters per cell. Longer macros are continued on the next line.
■ In order to prevent data and macro commands being confused, the cell under the specified macro instructions should be left empty. It is also possible to conclude a macro using the macro command {QUIT}.

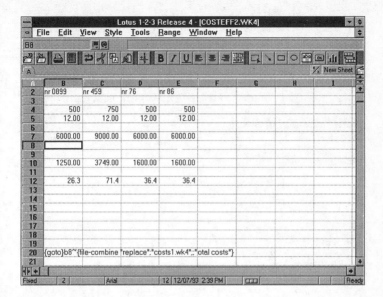

Macro worksheet

10.2.2 Assigning a name to the macro

Before a macro can be implemented, a name must be assigned to it which enables you to activate it easily. The name should also give an indication of the macro function. Assigning a name to a macro takes place in the same way as assigning a range name. In this case, the name is only assigned to the first cell and not to the entire macro range. Mark the cell and select the *Name* command from the *Range* menu.

Specify, in this dialog box, the name by means of which the macro is to be activated later. This can be done using a short key combination or a more lengthy name. There are, thus, two general possibilities:

■ Giving an extensive name to the macro, such as the name 'Total Costs'. This has the advantage that you can immediately recognize the macro at a later date.

The same restrictions apply to macro names as to range names (16 characters).

■ A short key combination enables you to activate the macro quickly and easily. First type a backslash and then a letter of your choice. In our example, this is \T. Only letters from A to Z may be chosen here.

Name dialog box

Thus, the procedure when assigning a name to a macro is as follows:

■ Using the cursor keys, go to the first cell where the macro is to be specified.

■ Open the *Range* menu and select the *Name* command.

■ Assign a name to the macro, for example, \T or Total Costs.

■ Execute the command by selecting Add and press Enter or activate OK.

In order to confirm the command and the specified range it is sufficient to activate only the starting position or the first cell of the total macro. Thus, it is not necessary to specify the whole range.

Now that the macro has been allocated a name, it can be used in conjunction with the worksheet. In order to be able to use the macro later, it is absolutely necessary

to save the worksheet using *File, Save*. Give the worksheet the name COSTEFF2.

Remarks concerning range names:

- Existing range names can be activated by selecting
  the *Name* option from the *Range* menu. A list of
  Existing Named Ranges is shown here.
- Range names can be removed by means of the
  Delete button in the *Name* dialog box.
- You can create a self-starting macro using the key
  combination \O.

10.2.3   Running a macro

When implementing a macro, use is made of a macro
letter or range name which has been allocated before-
hand. Depending on the method chosen when assigning a name, you can use either of two methods of activating a macro:

- If you are using a backslash and letter, the macro is
  activated by holding down the Ctrl key and pressing
  the assigned letter. In our example, that is T.
- If you have allocated a more extensive name to the
  macro, you can summon a list of all existing macro
  names using the key combination Alt-F3.

Macro Run window

In both cases, the values in the source worksheet COSTS1 are automatically transported to the worksheet COSTEFF2. The result is as follows:

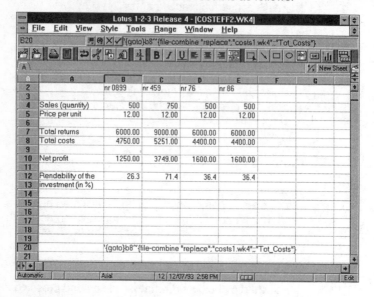

Worksheet after the macro

Notes:

- A macro is implemented by pressing the Ctrl key together with the allocated letter. The backslash is only used when the name is being assigned.
- A macro can be discontinued by pressing Ctrl-Pause.
- A macro can be altered later, if required, in the same way as labels.
- A long macro can be tested out step-by-step using the STEP function which is activated by pressing Alt-F2. Afterwards, you activate the macro as you would normally.

If a tested macro fulfils the function required, save it in the currently active file or in a separate file so that it can be used again later.

If an error occurs when a macro is being run, it is logical
to attempt to find the cause of the error first. The result
will often give an indication of what has gone wrong. If,
for instance, you have made a typing mistake when
specifying the macro, you only need to rectify this mistake in the macro command.

If the cause of the error is not directly obvious, use of
the the STEP function may provide the answer. This
function is activated by pressing Alt-F2. The word Step
appears on the status bar at the bottom of the screen.
After activating the macro, you can execute and check
each individual step by pressing a random key.

As soon as the cause of the error is found, activate the
relevant cell position and press F2. The mistake can
then be rectified.

10.3   Working with the macro recorder

Up until now we have entered the macro commands
one character at a time from the keyboard. The macro
recorder provides considerable simplification of this process. The program can record various commands automatically by means of this function. In the example
below, the same macro as previously will be recorded,
using the macro recorder this time. In this case, it is the
procedure which is important. First open the COST-
EFF1.WK4 worksheet and proceed as follows:

**Specify the cell in which the macro is to be re-
corded:**
Select a vacant row. Place the cell pointer on cell B19
for instance. The recording of the macro can now begin.

Making the macro definition:
Select the *Macro* option from the *Tools* menu. Select
the *Show Transcript* option from the subsequent dialog
window. Click on the Transcript title bar using the
mouse to activate this window, or press Alt-W to activate the *Window* menu and type the number in front of

Transcript. As you will see, the colour or shading of the title bar changes.

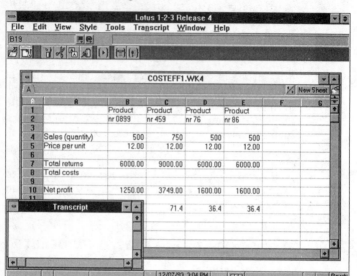

Removing keystrokes from the buffer:
There may already be keystrokes in the Transcript window. In order to avoid unpredictable results, any existing keystrokes should be removed. To do this, select the *Clear All* option from the *Edit* menu.

Recording keystrokes:
You can now begin recording the macro. Switch back to the worksheet, go to cell B19, and then select *Tools, Macro, Record*. The status bar displays the text Rec. Now enter the commands required to copy the Total Costs from the COST1.WK4 worksheet to the active worksheet. Macro definition is shown immediately in the worksheet. When this has been done, select *Tools, Macro, Stop Recording* to conclude the macro.

Examining the results of the keystrokes:
When you have executed all the commands, return to the Transcript window and examine the results of the

keystrokes. To do so, activate Transcript from the *Window* menu.

Adopting the result into the worksheet:
If you are satisfied with the result, adopt it into the worksheet in a vacant row, row 16 for instance. After marking the macro text, go to the *Edit* menu and select *Copy* or *Cut*. (The former makes a copy in the activated worksheet, the latter places the macro in the worksheet and removes it from the Transcript window.) Then switch to the worksheet and select the *Paste* option from the *Edit* menu. The result is shown below.

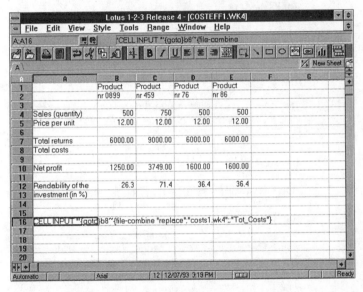

The macro is complete. Assign a name as described previously, and press Alt-F3 to try the macro out.

The advantage of this method of working is that you can use the contents of the Transcript window to copy macros to other worksheets or to create a different macro which only slightly deviates from this macro.

10.4   Macros including macros

The macros which we have created up until now have been executed fully from beginning to end. However, it is possible to interrupt the runthrough of a macro in order to enable the user to take certain decisions. This results in the so-called interactive macros.

It is also possible to extend the application of macros by including not only certain keystrokes, but also special commands in a macro. Accordingly, a small program can in fact be created to run ready-made applications for beginners.

Here are examples of possible macro commands:

a) Interactive commands

It is possible to enter relevant data during the execution of a macro by means of these commands. For instance:

macro command	function
{GET-NUMBER}	A number can be entered at the specified cell position.
{GET-LABEL}	A text can be entered at the specified cell position.
{GET-RANGE}	A range name or address can be entered in a dialog box; this is then entered in a cell as a number.

b) Commands to guide the runthrough of the program

It is possible to guide the program runthrough by means of logical commands. In this way, choice and repeat structures can be created.

macro command	function
{IF}	Checks the next precondition and thus makes it possible to include logical criteria in the macro.
{BRANCH}	Makes an unconditional jump in a macro to a specified location (this is interesting in the case of logical claims).
{DISPATCH}	Makes an indirect branch by transferring macro control to the cell whose name or address is specified.
{subroutine}	Enables you to use other macros as subroutines.
{RESTART}	Clears the subroutine stack, enabling the return to the main program.
{FOR}, {FORBREAK}	Used to create and end a loop (a repeatedly executed subroutine).
{QUIT}	Terminates the macro and returns to the 1-2-3/W window.

This list will make it clear that you can create macros with logical claims by specifying certain macro commands. It is also possible to create your own menus with special messages.

Exercise 10-2: A macro containing macro commands

Open the DEPREC.WK4 file. Construct a macro which first removes the range C3..C5 and any values contained and which then enables you to enter the data (purchase price, service life, salvage value) by means of a menu.

In order to carry out this exercise, the following steps must be implemented:

■ The range C3..C5 must be deleted.
■ The appropriate data should be entered.

The macro is to be recorded in cell F9 of the worksheet. The file containing this macro is to be saved under the name DEPMAC.WK4.

The following series of keystrokes removes the relevant range and operates the data input:

keystroke	function
{HOME}	Moves to the first cell of the worksheet
{GOTO}	Activates the GoTo command
C3	Specifies the appropriate cell position
~	Executes the command
{ANCHOR}	Activates the range specification key
{DOWN}	Cursor down one position
{DOWN}	Cursor down another position
~	Executes the command
{DEL}	Deletes the cell contents in the range
{GOTO}	Activates the GoTo command
C3	specifies the appropriate cell position
{GETNUMBER "Enter Purchase Price";C3}~	
	Enters the specified cost price at the relevant cursor position
{DOWN}	Moves the cursor down one position
{GETNUMBER "Enter Service Life";C4}~	
	Enters the specified service life at the relevant cursor position
{DOWN}	Moves the cursor down one position
{GETNUMBER "Enter residual value";C5}~	
	Enters the specifies salvage value at the relevant cursor position
{QUIT}	Terminates the macro

Enter the entire macro as a label, as shown in the figure on the following page.

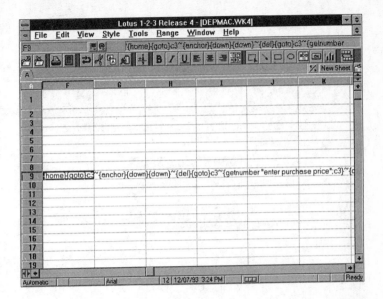

Macro text

The next step is to assign a name to the macro. Open the *Range* menu and select the *Name* option. Type the abbreviation \E in the dialog box. Save the macro under the name DEPMAC.WK4. You can subsequently activate the macro by typing Ctrl-E. The initial result will be as shown on the following page.

The figure shows that the values which had been entered to calculate the depreciation have been deleted. Accordingly, ERR is displayed in the other cells. A dialog box appears in which you should specify the cost price. When the cost price has been entered, the other values can be specified successively. Then the program will return to the worksheet automatically.

In this example, we have applied various commands in order to familiarize you with the working procedure. In principle, the macro in the example can be formulated much more easily by replacing the first section from

{HOME} to {DEL} by the command {BLANK C3..C5}.
Try this out.

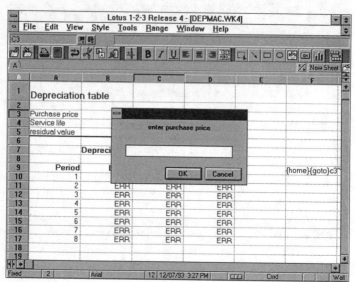

Macro in uitvoering

10.5   Compiling a macro library

Up until now, we have recorded macro worksheets and
stored them in files along with the worksheets. However, in order to be able to use a macro with various
files, it is possible to compile a separate macro library.
In this case, the macros are stored in a separate file.

Summary of chapter 10

■ Use of macros can considerably alleviate working
with 1-2-3/W if certain procedures have to be repeated. Common applications for macros are: auto-
mating series of commands which are frequently

used, implementing a procedure which repeats itself and the construction of a personal worksheet.

■ Before beginning a macro, you must formulate exactly what you expect from the macro. In addition, a macro which has been constructed must be carefully tested.

■ Menu instructions, special keys and specified cell data may be included in a macro.

■ The macro must be recorded in an empty range in the worksheet.

■ You assign a name to a macro by selecting the *Name* option from the *Range* menu. Type a backslash followed by a letter, for example, \E in the appropriate text box.

■ The macro is activated by pressing the Ctrl key simultaneously with the assigned letter. The key combination Alt-F3 produces a list of all defined macros.

■ It is possible to create macros which resemble small-scale programs by applying certain macro commands.

11   Charts and diagrams

11.1   Survey of the graphic possibilities

1-2-3/W enables you to create *business graphics* from existing numeric values.

The point of departure here is the orderly display of data and results in tables for planning and presentation. The objective of business graphics programs is to convert the numerical data into line, bar and pie charts. Business graphics are applied to the following areas of management and administration in particular:

(a) management
   - graphically processing diverse data
   - presentation of results

(b) finance and administration
   - internal company reports
   - comparison of estimated and real results
   - analysis of current developments

(c) sales/marketing/advertising
   - analysis of sales development (comparison with estimated figures, preliminary forecasts)
   - diverse forms of presentation
   - brochures

(d) production/material policy
   - calculation of relevant data
   - points of departure in production planning
   - display of technical data (measuring/test data)

(e) staff policy
   - analysis of personnel
   - assistance in staff planning

Various benefits are connected to the use of business graphics in the areas mentioned. For the decision-makers at management level in particular, they can provide welcome assistance in the execution of their work. Charts give a quicker and clearer survey of relevant data than lists and tables in the traditional style. Complex relationships are also easier to understand, important information can be made more conspicuous and, thus, is retained longer. Department managers and heads of sales, marketing and financial planning can benefit from these business graphics, due to a better documentation of results and the possibility of formulating reports more rapidly and cheaply.

11.2 Types of charts and diagrams and their variants

The existing data form the starting point for graphics in 1-2-3/W. In this, the numerical data in this worksheet can be converted into different types of charts and diagrams.

Each program which creates business graphics contains a certain amount of variants. The following types are available in 1-2-3/W. The choice of type depends on the application:

chart type	description/application
line diagram/ 3D line diagram	Separate points are joined by a line; this is specially suited to display developments with the passage of time.
area chart/ 3D area chart	Various data ranges are displayed on top of one another; the individual data points are linked to one another by lines; the areas between the lines are filled in using different colours and shading.
bar chart/ 3D bar chart	Bar charts make it possible to place different series of information next to one another; in addition to the display of time-oriented developments, these are very suited to the comparison of values in similar groups of

	data; display is also possible in horizontal or tiled form.
XY chart	This serves to clarify the relation between a unit X and a unit Y.
HLCO chart	Enables the display of temporary swings by indicating the highest, lowest, closing and opening values.
mixed	Bars and lines are displayed together in one chart; this is especially suited to showing different data types in one chart.
radar	Each data range is displayed on its own axis which begins at the centre; particularly suited to a rapid display of the data points which deviate from the mainstream.

In the *Chart* menu (which appears when you have chosen a chart, see below) you can use the *Type* option to activate a dialog window which enables you to switch between the various forms of charts and diagrams. You can also switch between horizontal and vertical display. However, the quickest and easiest method of switching between forms is to use the SmartIcons set. As soon as you have selected a chart, the SmartIcons set is adjusted to contain icons specifically suited to charts.

The diverse charts can be supplemented with relevant information and texts, such as:

■ headers and subtitles
■ suitable names for the axes
■ legends
■ value tables

In addition, there are specific functions for giving various diagrams a certain layout, for example, with shading and line patterns, colours and letter types.

11.3 Procedure when constructing a chart

When constructing a chart in 1-2-3/W, proceed as follows:

- Enter a series of values in a worksheet and mark the range required for the creation of the chart.
- Specify the area where the chart is to be located.
- Specify the type of chart (change the chart type, define the parameters, make additions).
- Save the worksheet containing the chart.

We shall use the following exercise to become familiar will these manoeuvres.

Exercise 11-1: Creating a simple chart

In a company, the development of the returns over the last eight years are to be presented in chart form. The values are as follows:

year	returns x £1 million
1985	120
1986	102
1987	105
1988	128
1989	137
1990	154
1991	156
1992	166

a) Create a line diagram which shows the development of these returns. The diagram is allocated the name LINE1.
b) Save the worksheet containing the diagram under the name SUCCESS1.WK4.

11.3.1   Input of data for the diagram

To construct a diagram, the required data must be entered in a worksheet. Therefore, type the data in the
worksheet first. Remember that the years should be entered as text and not as numeric values. The screen
then appears as follows:

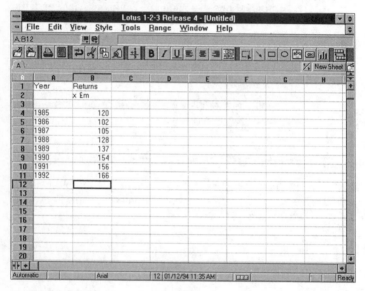

Values for the chart

Now select the range containing the data which are to
be displayed in chart form, in our case A4..B11. This
range contains the cells with the values which are to be
displayed and also the labels in the worksheet which
are to be shown in the diagram.

When defining a range for the chart, the following points
apply:

■ The data in the first column of the worksheet (text,
years) are the so-called X data. If diagrams with axes

are to be displayed, these data are used as titles for the axes.

■ The other columns represent the data ranges. They are internally referred to as A to W; they contain the ranges for the numeric data to be graphically displayed.

11.3.2 Summoning Chart

In order to create a new chart, open the *Tools* menu after selecting the appropriate range. Select the *Chart* option. The arrow pointer changes into a graphic symbol which enables you to define the size of the chart. Make the chart just the right size to fit onto the screen alongside the data. The result should look something like this:

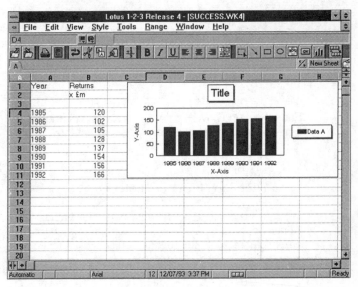

Keep the following points in mind:

- The chart does not yet really conform to our wishes; this is because it has been contructed using the 1-2-3/W default settings.
- The name 'CHART 1' appears on the Edit line. You can adopt this name but you may also alter it if you wish.
- When the chart is displayed on the screen, the *Range* menu changes to *Chart* on the menu bar. The Smart-Icon set changes too.

Change the name of the chart by selecting the *Name* option from the *Chart* menu. The following dialog box appears:

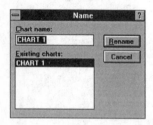

Enter the name LINE1 in the Chart Name box and press Enter. This name subsequently appears at the top left-hand corner.

11.3.3   Specifying the chart parameters

In order to create a graph from particular values in a worksheet, you must specify certain parameters of the graph to conform to the required objectives. These concern:

- determining the form of the chart
- defining the data ranges
- specific instructions for the chart layout (titles, axes texts and legends).

Specifying the range

In order to become more acquainted with working with charts and diagrams in 1-2-3/W, first open the *Chart* menu and select the *Ranges* option. The following dialog window appears on the screen:

Range dialog box

The currently valid ranges are displayed. The first range is used for the X axis labels. The information located in this range is placed at regular intervals along the horizontal axis of the chart or diagram by the program. The letters A to W are used to designate the various ranges, the *data sets*. There are thus 23 different data sets possible which can be applied when constructing a chart. Specify the range as you would do in the worksheet, using cell addresses or range names.

In our example, the development of the returns is to be displayed in a bar chart. When creating charts, the data which are to be used as X axis labels under the X axis have to be defined. In this case, these are the years from 1985 to 1992. There is only one further data range; this is registered as Series A - Data A.

Since you have already selected the required ranges, these will already be displayed in the Range box.

Regardless of this example, the following facilities are available for determining data ranges:

- Ranges can be extracted from three-dimensional worksheets.
- The data range need not apply to the currently active file; this may be a file on harddisk or diskette.

Specifying the type of chart

The choice of the type of chart is, of course, elementary. The default suggestion, Bar, can easily be altered. Open the *Chart* menu and select *Type*. The following dialog box appears:

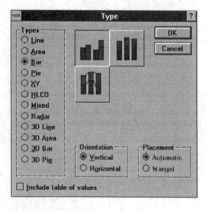

Type dialog box

The figure shows the basic types of charts and diagrams which can be created in 1-2-3/W. In addition, you can choose either Vertical or Horizontal orientation and specify whether or not a table of values is to be included.

The bar chart is the default setting in the *Type* dialog box. We shall create a line diagram in our example, because this type of graph is well suited to the display of changing numerical values with the passage of time. Accordingly, activate the Line option button.

Specifying titles for a chart

The chart can be given a title and the axes can display information to help clarify the chart. This information is registered using the *Headings* option from the *Chart* menu. The *Headings* dialog box looks like this:

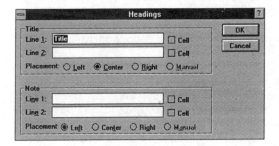

To implement our exercise, type the title 'Development of the Returns' in the Title Line 1 text box. You can specify a second title in Line 2 if you wish, but that is not necessary here. Both titles are normally displayed centred above the chart, the first title being larger than the second. If you wish to align the text left or right, select the relevant option button. If a text in a cell is to be used as the title, activate cell (Tab or click) and then specify the cell in the Title Line 1 or 2 box. It is also possible to display the second title in a different font. We shall return to this topic later.

Axis titles

It is advisable to allocate a description to the axes. To do this, activate the *Axis* option from the *Chart* menu. When you have chosen the X-Axis option from the subsequent submenu, activate the Cell check box next to Axis title and then type A1 in the text box. Then press

Enter. The text contained in cell A1 (Year) will now be displayed centred under the X axis. Do the same for the Y axis in the submenmu but now type the text which is displayed in the cells B1 and B2. This text will be displayed to the left of the actual chart.

11.3.4 Displaying a chart on the screen

When all information for the chart has been entered, you can reproduce it on the screen and on the printer.

Displaying the chart on the entire screen

Normally, the chart does not fill the whole screen. You can adjust the size of the chart by means of the small blocks at the sides of the chart frame. Drag the block at the lower left-hand side of the chart to the bottom left-hand corner of the screen. The screen should look like this:

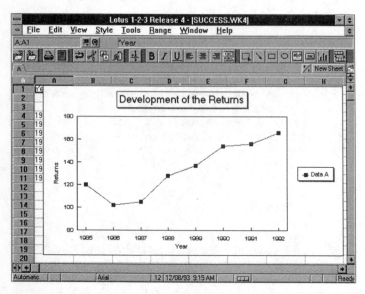

Parallel display of worksheet and chart

When the chart is located in the worksheet, this provides the advantage that if the values in the worksheet are altered, those in the chart are automatically adjusted. Try this out by altering the value of one of the montly figures.

The worksheet and chart are saved together by selecting the *Save* command from the *File* menu.

11.4 Line diagram with various ranges

The line diagram is particularly useful for displaying time-related data. This allows ready comparison between various aspects such as the development of returns and costs. We shall outline this using the following exercise:

Exercise 11-2: Create a line diagram using various ranges

With reference to the previous example, the costs were subject to the following development over the same period of time:

year	returns x £1 million
1985	98
1986	110
1987	102
1988	103
1989	113
1990	125
1991	130
1992	137

Enter the costs in the 1-2-3/W worksheet SUC-
CESS1.WK4 and then place the returns and the costs
opposite each other in a line diagram. Save the chart
under the name LINE2. Save the worksheet under the
name SUCCESS2.WK4.

11.4.1   Creating and adopting different ranges

If we wish to compare the returns and the costs, we
must first enter the costs in the SUCCESS1 file. Load
the file using the *Open* command from the *File* menu
and enter the cost data in column C. The worksheet will
appear as follows:

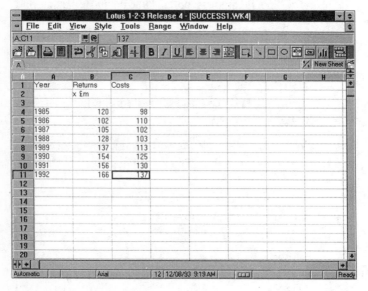

Worksheet containing data for the diagram

Then mark the range A4..C11 and select the *Chart* option from the *Tools* menu. Then place the cell pointer in
D1 and drag the frame to the bottom right-hand corner
of cell H19. There are now two data ranges. This can be

seen if you select the *Ranges* option from the *Chart* menu. The result is the following dialog window:

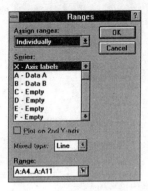

Costs and returns can be shown simultaneously in one chart, enabling easy comparison.

The title of the chart must now be changed to 'Costs/Returns Development'. This takes place in the usual way via the *Titles* option from the *Chart* menu. The titles of the X and Y axes should be altered to 'Years' and 'In £ million' respectively. The type of chart should be altered from the default bar setting to line diagram.

This should produce a perfect overview.

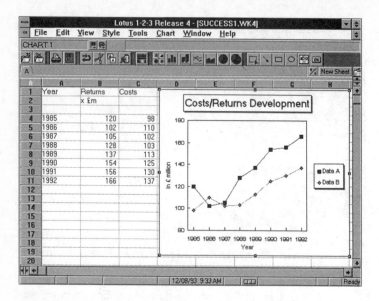

Line diagram with various ranges

11.4.2   Adding a legend

Because two ranges are now being shown, in the form of two lines, it is advisable to add a legend for better orientation. This clarifies the significance of the two lines in the chart, i.e. which line displays the returns figures and which line the costs. Normally a legend is shown in the chart but the information has yet to be specified.

Select the *Legend* option from the *Chart* menu and enter the information as shown in the dialog box on the following page.

Press Enter or click on OK in order to place the legend automatically at the right of the chart. The symbol used indicates the relevant line in the chart.

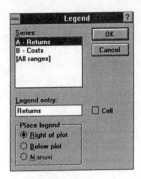

Legend dialog box

11.4.3 Changing the line format

It is possible to format the lines in a certain way in line diagrams, XY, HLCO and mixed charts. This takes place using the *Lines & Color* option from the *Style* menu. First select the line you wish to alter and open the dialog box.

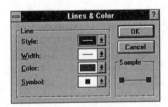

Lines & Color dialog box

The options have the following significance:

Style Select the line style from the pull-down menu, for instance a dotted line or a broken line. None means that no line will be shown.

Width Select the line thickness from this puli-down menu.

Color   This option activates the colour palette
               from which you can choose the required
               line colour.

Symbol   The pull-down list provides a number of
               symbols to indicate the data points. If you
               wish to alter the default display, select a
               different symbol here.

For instance, create a point diagram display by first selecting the line in the diagram by clicking on it and then
selecting *Style, Lines & Color, Line None*. The result is
as follows:

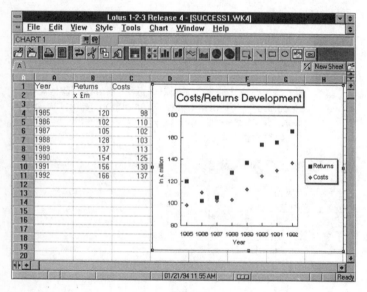

Point diagram

Subsequently return to the original settings.

11.4.4 Adding gridlines

In order to connect certain values to one another more quickly when viewing a chart, it can be very useful to add gridlines to the chart. This is possible using the *Grids* option from the *Chart* menu. The following dialog box appears:

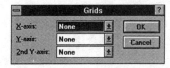

Grids dialog box

This box indicates that normally no gridlines are shown. The options shown here have the following significance:

option	significance
X-axis	This pull-down menu provides the options, None, Major interval, Minor interval and Both. If you select any one except None, horizontal gridlines are reproduced in the chart on the screen and on the printer.
Y-axis	This pull-down menu also provides the options None, Major interval, Minor interval and Both. If you select any one except None, vertical gridlines will be shown in the chart on the screen and on the printer.
2nd Y-axis	This pull-down menu also provides the options None, Major interval, Minor interval and Both. If you select any one except none, vertical gridlines will be reproduced in the chart on the screen and on the printer.

If you select gridlines for both the X and the Y axis, both horizontal and vertical gridlines will be shown in the

chart. Try this out using the Minor interval option. The
result will appear as follows:

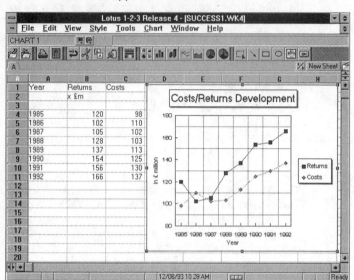

Line diagram with gridlines

Subsequently switch off the grid options once more.

11.4.5   Using Data Labels

Another method of explaining the lines is to supply the
individual points in the chart with their corresponding
values. To do this, select the *Data Labels* option from
the *Chart* menu. You must specify the relevant range
there: for A that is B4..B11 and for B that is C4..C11.

It is possible to locate the labels at one of five different
positions in relation to the data points: Center, Right,
Below, Left or Above. In both cases, select the display
option Below. You can also extend the chart a little to
improve legibility.

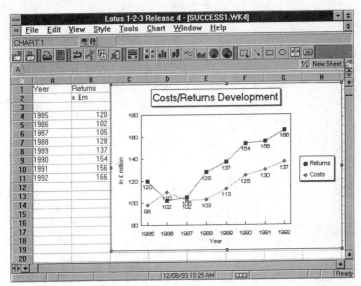

Line diagram with Data labels

As you will observe, the program places the data labels in the line diagram exactly under the data points.

Save the worksheet under the name SUCCESS2.WK4.

A variant of this is the allocation of a table of values. Remove the data labels (*Chart, Data Labels, Range of labels*, press Del) and select the *Type* option from the *Chart* menu. Activate the Include Table of Values option at the bottom of the dialog box. The information is summarized under the chart.

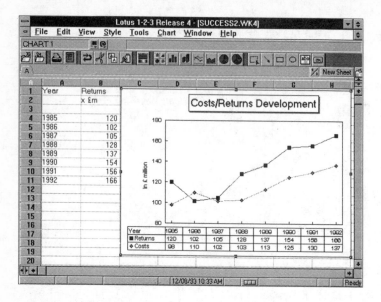

Line diagram with Table of Values

11.5   Creating and designing bar charts

We shall use an existing worksheet to create a bar
chart. In the case of the line diagram, we have seen that
the values needed to create a chart must be contained
in a worksheet. Thus, it is obvious that an existing worksheet may be used to construct a chart.

We shall use the following exercise to become acquainted with bar charts:

**Exercise 11-3: Create bar charts with different ran-
ges, and also in stacked form**

Load the TURNOVR5.WK4 file containing the real and
estimated figures for the twelve months of the year.

a) Create a bar chart in which the real and estimated

figures are represented by adjacent vertical bars. Save the diagram under the name BAR1.
b) Subsequently save the worksheet under the name TURNOVR5.WK4.

A bar chart with different ranges is created in the same way as a line diagram. The procedure is as follows, when you have loaded the file TURNOVR5.WK4 using the *Open* command from the *File* menu:

Specifying the ranges

You must first mark the range A5..B16 in the currently active worksheet. This range is to be adopted in the new diagram. Then select *Chart* option from the *Tools* menu. Make the frame for the diagram large enough to fill the entire screen. Then select *Name* from the *Chart* menu and specify the name BAR1 for the diagram. Now specify the other ranges by selecting the *Ranges* option from the *Chart* menu. Activate the B Series and move to the Range box. Complete the dialog window as follows:

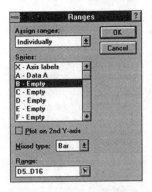

Confirm the command by pressing Enter. The X range is used for the titles along the X axis and the program uses the A and B ranges for the bar display. Accordingly, for each data series, a bar can be made with a special colour or shading since each bar corresponds to a value in the series.

Specifying titles

A bar chart supplies little information without a title
above the chart and information along the axes. The definition of titles is just the same when working with bar
charts as with line diagrams. For the texts, the procedure is as follows in our example:

- Open the *Chart* menu and select the *Headings* option.
- Type 'Comparison of estimated/real returns' in the
  first text box.
- Go to the second box using Tab or the mouse and
  type 'Shylock Ltd.'
- Press Enter to confirm.

In order to specify the titles of the axes, select the *Axis*
option and then successively X-Axis and Y-Axis. Enter
the following data in the respective text boxes.

- for the X-Axis title: 'Months'
- for the Y-Axis title: 'in £ thousands'.

Adding legends

Because two data ranges will be included in the diagram, it is necessary to add an explanatory legend. This
clarifies the pattern or colouring used in the diagram.
The procedure with legends is also similar to that of the
line diagrams:

- Open the *Chart* menu and select the *Legend* option.
- For the A Series, type the word 'Estimated ' in the
  Legend Entry box.
- Activate the B Series and type the word 'Real' in the
  Legend Entry box.
- Click on OK or press Enter to confirm the specifica-
  tions.

Displaying the chart

The chart will now appear as follows:

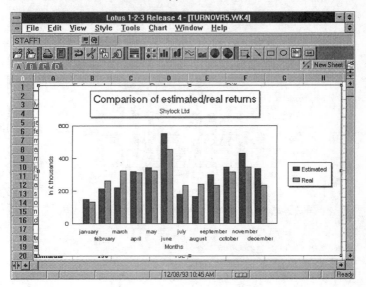

Bar Chart

The individual bars representing the estimated and real returns are displayed vertically. The names of the months are shown under the X axis.

Adding gridlines and data values to bar charts

We shall now add gridlines to the bar chart. Open the *Chart* menu and select the *Grids* option. Select the option Both from the Y-axis pull-down menu. Gridlines appear across the chart.

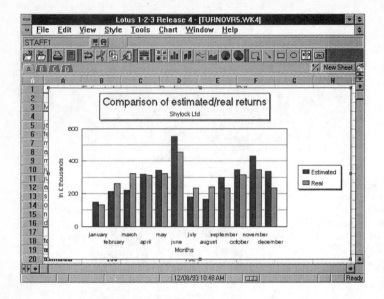

Bar chart with horizontal gridlines

Data values can also be displayed in the bar chart by
means of the *Data Labels* option from the *Chart* menu.
Specify the relevant range in the Range of Labels box.
In this case, you could place the texts above the appropriate bars for instance. If there are negative values, the
program places the values under the relevant bars.

Scale distribution
1-2-3/W automatically makes a scale distribution and
numeration along the axes in a way that all data can be
displayed. An alternative distribution can be specified
using the *Axis* option from the *Chart* menu. The submenu displays the X-Axis, Y-Axis and 2nd Y-Axis options.
Try out the Y-Axis option in our example. The corresponding dialog window appears.

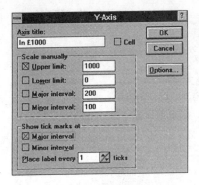

It is possible to have the scaling done automatically or to do it yourself. Specify the required scaling in the Scale Manually box. Specify 1000 as the upper limit and observe the difference with the original display. Subsequently, switch this option off again to return to the original settings.

Note: 1-2-3/W 1-2-3 ignores a positive lower limit and a negative upper limit for the X axis. Accordingly, you are assured of zero being included in the scale distribution.

If you first select the figures shown in the chart by clicking on them, you can then alter the layout by selecting the *Number Format* option from the *Style* menu.

Applying colours and shading

The Options command enables you to vary the colouring or, in the case of a monochrome monitor, the pattern or shading.

First select the bars by clicking on them. Then choose *Lines & Color* from the *Style* menu. The corresponding dialog window appears.

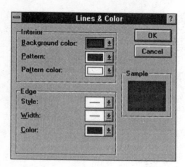

You can now choose the desired colours for the data ranges.

Applying shading takes place in the same way.

11.6 Designing and creating a pie chart

1-2-3/W is able to display pie charts which are particularly suitable for the display of parts of a whole. The Pie is the whole, divided into various segments. The pie chart is not suited to the comparison of various data ranges or display of a large number of data points.

We shall illustrate the usage and possibilities of the pie chart using an exercise:

Exercise 11-4: Designing and creating a pie chart

a) Load the worksheet TURNOVR2.WK4, made in a previous exercise, which contains real returns for the individual months of the year.
b) Using these values, make a normal pie chart. Allocate the name CIRCLE to this chart.
c) Save the file under the name CIRCLES.WK4.

In a pie chart, the X range is used to represent the labels for the legend. The A data series represents the segment values. If segments have to be emphasized or displayed in a different colour, this is done in the B data series. If you wish to use a series to register additional segment labels, do this using the C data series.

To begin, load the TURNOVR2 worksheet. Mark the range A4..B15. Then select the *Chart* option from the *Tools* menu and draw a frame for the chart, large enough to fill the screen. Select the *Name* option from the *Chart* menu and specify the name 'Circle'. Then select the *Type* option from the *Chart* menu. Choose Pie.

Now add a two-line title by selecting the *Headings* option from the *Chart* menu. Type the titles as follows:

First title: Specification of returns per month
Second title: (1992)

The result appears as follows:

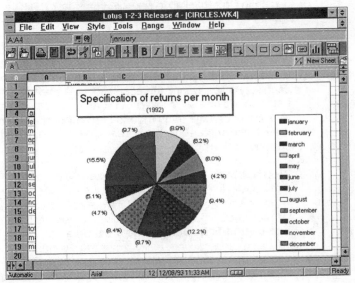

Pie chart

As you see, the percentages are calculated automatically and shown adjacent to the corresponding segment. The data from the first series are used as legend titles.

Segments of a pie chart can also be given special colouring or shading. To do this, select the segment in question and then select the *Lines & Color* option from the *Style* menu.

A very useful facility consists of emphasizing a certain segment by lifting it out of the pie. The easiest way of doing this is to click on it and drag it out the required distance.

11.7   Creating XY charts

XY charts are similar to line diagrams in certain respects. In these, the X range defines the X co-ordinates. The Y co-ordinates are the values which are allocated to the ranges A to W. Each pair of XY co-ordinates determines a data point which is generally displayed as a symbol. These charts are particularly useful in cases where representation of dependence between two units is required. An example of this is the dependence of the returns on the advertising costs or the interwoven relationship between consumption and savings patterns.

We shall carry out the following exercise to become familiar with the creation of XY charts.

Exercise 11-5: Designing and creating an XY chart

Create an XY chart which displays the relationship between consumption expenditure and saving, depending on the available income.

income	expenditure	savings
0	20	-20
50	60	-10
100	100	0
150	140	10
200	180	20

a) Enter the data in a 1-2-3/W worksheet.

b) Subsequently, create an XY chart with the following titles:

Main title: Consumption and savings function
X axis: Income
Y axis: Consumption/Savings

c) Enter the values at the appropriate points.

d) Save the file under the name XYCHART.WK4.

Of course, the table must first be constructed in a 1-2-3/W worksheet. That will appear as follows:

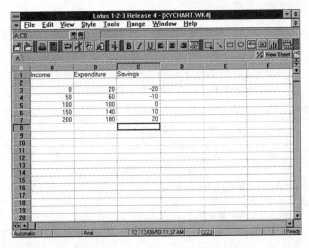

Table for XY chart

Creating an XY chart is similar to constructing a line diagram. The most important difference is that, in the case of an XY chart, the X axis is not an explanation, but always contains number values. The procedure in the example is as follows:

Specify the ranges

Mark the range A3..C7 in the worksheet and select the *Chart* option from the *Tools* menu. Select an area for the chart. The result is a bar chart in which the following data apply to the ranges:

A range: A3..A7
B range: B3..B7
C range: C3..C7

Selecting the type of chart

Alter the type of chart in the next stage. Go to the *Type* option in the *Chart* menu. Activate the XY option in the subsequent dialog box.

Defining titles

Select the *Headings* option from the *Chart* menu. Type 'Consumption and savings pattern' in the first text box. Press Enter.

Select *Axis* from the *Chart* menu. Specify 'Income' for the X Axis and 'Consumption/Saving' for the Y Axis.

Adding a legend

Since there are two data ranges in the chart, it is necessary to add some clarification. Select *Legend* from the *Chart* menu and specify the B and C Series.

- for Series B: Consumption in the Legend entry box
- for Series C: Savings in the Legend entry box.

Adding data values to the XY chart

Data values can also be shown in an XY chart. This takes place using the *Data Labels* option from the *Chart* menu, in which you can specify the corresponding data ranges (here B3..B7 and C3..C7). Place the labels above the lines in this example.

The result should look like this:

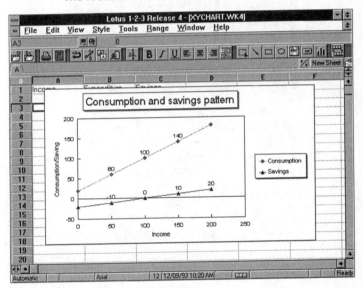

The XY chart

Save the result.

11.8   Creating an Area chart

Another basic type of chart is the Area chart. This resembles the line diagram to a certain extent. In the area
chart, the areas between the individual lines are emphasized by various colours, patterns or shading. This
leads to a more attractive presentation.

There are several useful application areas for area
charts. They are normally used to show time-oriented
data. For example:

■ the development of quantities
■ components of an accumulated statistical unit within
   a certain period
■ extent of trend swings within the period
■ usage of available capacity.

Exercise 11-6: Create an area chart

In a company which deals in three different products,
there is an overall increase in turnover. It is the products B
and C which are generally responsible for this increase.
An area chart is to show the individual and the total development of the turnover within a certain period of time.

The turnover figures are as follows:

year	product A	product B	product C
1983	80	102	180
1984	75	104	145
1985	85	108	122
1986	77	134	140
1987	80	183	199
1988	75	204	255
1989	72	253	277
1990	70	280	313
1991	72	290	300
1992	72	310	350

Exercises:

a) Create an area chart using these figures. Assign the title 'Turnover growth continues'.
b) Allocate the following titles to the X and Y axes:
   X Axis: 'Years'
   Y Axis: 'in £ million'
c) Specify the following data:
   A: product A
   B: product B
   C: product C
d) Save the worksheet as AREA.WK4.

First adopt the figures into a new worksheet. Then proceed as follows:

Defining the ranges

Mark the range A3..D12 in the worksheet and select the *Chart* option from the *Tools* menu. Draw a frame for the chart. The result is a bar chart. Select the *Ranges* option from the *Chart* menu and enter the following data in the Range box after activating the corresponding Series:

Series X: Range A3..A12
Series A: Range B3..B12
Series B: Range C3..C12
Series C: Range D3..D12

Press Enter to confirm.

Selecting the type of chart

Now alter the type of chart. Select *Type* from the *Chart* menu and choose Area from the options presented.

Specifying titles

Now select the *Headings* option from the *Chart* menu and type in the first text box 'Turnover growth continues'.

Specify the axis titles using the *Axis* option from the *Chart* menu:

- for the X axis: Years
- for the Y axis: In £ million.

Adding a legend

Unfortunately the standard data in the legend are not yet very informative. We shall alter this. Select the *Legend* option from the *Chart* menu and specify the following:

- for Series A: product A at Legend entry
- for Series B: product B
- for Series C: product C

This should produce the following chart:

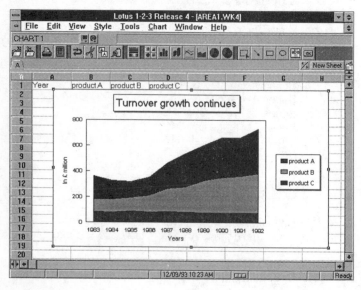

The Area chart

11.9 Creating an HLCO chart

HLCO charts provide a good overview of fluctuation in values. Accordingly, you can easily examine the course of shares or foreign currency or the swings in the market values of goods.

HLCO charts are a special form of vertical bar charts. Each bar or each vertical line may represent one or more aspects of price fluctuation over a certain period of time (one month or one day, for instance). These are the maximum and minimum values. The opening and closing values can also be represented.

Example: A chart is to be created in order to provide an analysis of the maximum and minimum share values in a certain month.

We shall use the following exercise in order to illustrate how HLCO charts are created.

Exercise 11-7: Create an HLCO chart

In order to make an analysis of share values, the share indices are to be registered for a particular share for each separate month. An HLCO chart is to display the course.

month	highest	lowest	closing	opening
Jan	102	80	95	100
Feb	104	75	99	95
Mar	108	85	104	99
Apr	144	77	104	104
May	149	102	110	104
June	152	108	115	110
July	149	110	120	115
Aug	140	75	77	120
Sep	145	100	122	116
Oct	155	104	122	122
Nov	156	111	126	122
Dec	155	120	145	126

Exercises:

a) Enter these data in a worksheet and create an HLCO
   chart along with the following texts:
   - title: Development of the share index
   - subtitle: Shylock Ltd.
   - title of the X axis: Months
   - title of the Y axis: Share value
b) Save the worksheet as SHARE1.WK4.

The figures shown above must first be adopted into the
worksheet in the columns A to E. This is the basis of the
chart.

Specifying the ranges

Mark the range A3..E14 and select the *Chart* option
from the *Tools* menu. Draw a frame where the chart is
to be located in the worksheet. The result is a bar chart.
Open the *Ranges* option from the *Chart* menu and
specify the following data at the appropriate places
using Tab and cursor or the mouse:

Series X-Axis labels: Range A3..A14
Series A: Range B3..B14
Series B: Range C3..C14
Series C: Range D3..D14
Series D: Range E3..E14

Selecting the type of chart

Now alter the type of chart. Select *Type* from the *Chart*
menu and activate the HLCO option.

Specifying the titles

Now select *Headings* from the *Chart* menu and type
'Development of the share index'. Type 'Shylock Ltd.' in
the second text box.

You can specify the axis titles using the *Axis* option from the *Chart* menu:

■ for the X axis: Months
■ for the Y axis: Share value.

Removing a legend

A legend is not really useful in an HLCO chart. There-fore we shall now remove it from this example.
Select the legend by clicking on it and pressing the Del key.

The result should appear as follows:

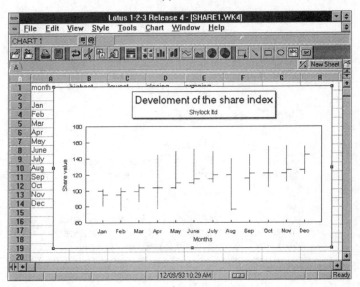

The HLCO chart

The chart illustrates that the highest and lowest value for each month are shown as a straight vertical line. The length of the line indicates the fluctuation.

■ If the line is short, there has been little price fluctuation.

■ If the line is long, there has been considerable price fluctuation.

Our example shows that there has been substantial fluctuation in the months of April and August. In contrast, January and March indicate little movement.

In addition, the closing values are indicated by a horizontal stripe to the right and the opening values by a stripe to the left. Accordingly, the difference between opening and closing values is obvious.

The following range settings are automatically applied in HLCO charts:

X Series: Range A3..A14
High value as A range: B3..B14
Low value as B range: C3..C14
Closing values as C range: D3..D14
Opening values as D range: E3..E14

11.10 Creating mixed charts

It is also possible to create a mixed form of lines and bars in 1-2-3/W. This type of chart a very suitable for illustrating a certain trend by means of a line through a bar chart.

When you have entered the required information in a worksheet and marked it, select the *Chart* option from the *Tools* menu. Draw a frame for the chart. A bar diagram appears. Define the relevant ranges and axes using the *Ranges* and *Axis* options from the *Chart* menu. Then go to the *Chart* menu and select *Type*. Activate the Mixed option. You can select one of the six types of mixed chart by clicking on it or by pressing Tab and the cursor keys and Enter.

11.11 Chart drawings

If you have a mouse, You may wish to embellish your charts with some graphic work or attract special attention to a particular area. You may wish to use the special drawing facilities provided by 1-2-3/W.

Open the *Tools* menu and select the *Draw* option. A submenu appears from which you can choose graphic options.

- Line: enables you, by holding the left mouse button and dragging, to draw a line in the chart or diagram.
- Polyline: enables to draw a number of lines attached to one another. To terminate the line, double click on the left mouse button.
- Arrow: enables you to draw an arrow in the worksheet or in the chart or from one to the other to illustrate certain data.
- Rectangle: enables you to draw a rectangle to enclose certain data. Drag it across the required area. It can be enlarged or reduced by clicking on the black peripheral points and dragging.
- Rounded rectangle: as with Rectangle but the corners are rounded.
- Arc: enables you to draw a bent line.
- Ellipse: enables you to draw an ellipse by dragging the mouse across the required area.
- Polygon: enables you to draw a multi-sided figure. Hold the mouse button down to draw a line. Each time you click a new line will begin. Double click to terminate the figure. The program automatically draws the ultimate joining line.
- Freehand: enables you to draw a figure as long as the mouse button is held down.
- Text: enables you to draw a box in which you can enter text directly. This is very useful for describing certain points of a worksheet or chart.
- Button: enables you to place a macro button in the worksheet or chart. You can specify the macro which is to be activated from this button.

Summary of chapter 11

■ Business graphics can be created in 1-2-3/W. This involves translating numeric values into comprehen-
sible images. The important benefits gained by using
business graphics lie in the improved documentation
of results and direct explanation of complex issues. It
is also possible to create your own free-hand graphic
images.

■ In 1-2-3/W it is possible to create line, bar, area, XY,
HLCO, radar and pie charts. When compiling business graphics, it is important to select the appropriate
type of chart for a correct expression of the data.

■ There are diverse options to improve the chart display. This involves the addition of titles and legends,
and the application of shading, colouring and scaling
to enhance the presentation.

■ The data which are necessary to create the chart already exist in a worksheet or must be specified before creating the chart.

■ The chart is created via the *Chart* option from the
Tools menu. When the *Chart* menu becomes available, the *Type* option from this menu enables you to
select the required type of chart: Line, Area, Bar, Pie,
XY, HLCO, Mixed, Radar and the various three-
dimensional forms of these.

■ The range data determine the values in the creation
of the chart. The *Headings* option from the *Chart*
menu enables you to assign titles to the chart. There
are two lines for chart titles. The *Axis* option from the
Chart menu enables you to do the same for the axes.

■ Gridlines can be displayed by means of the *Grids* option from the *Chart* menu. In general, this benefits the
legibility of the chart.

■ 1-2-3/W has two variants of the bar chart: the normal
form and the stacked bar chart. In the normal form,
the data are displayed adjacent to one another while
in the stacked form the bars are placed on top of one
another. You may also choose to connect the bars in
a stacked bar chart using comparison lines.

■ A pie chart is particularly suited to expressing segments of a whole. In a pie chart, the X Series is used

as the legend. The A Series contains the relevant values.

■ An XY diagram is especially suited to showing inter-dependence between units. In the XY diagram, the X Series displays the X co-ordinates, and the values which are assigned to the A to W Series are used as the Y co-ordinates. In the XY diagram, each XY pair of co-ordinates expresses a data point which is generally displayed as a symbol.

12   Data management

The third basic function in 1-2-3/W concerns data management. This enables you to manage data files flexibly. In this chapter, several basic concepts will be dealt with first and then a description will be given of the way a database is compiled. There will also be an extensive explanation of how to search for records which satisfy certain criteria. In addition, versatile analysis and sorting options will be discussed in the light of examples.

12.1   The possibilities of database programs

A database can be regarded as an extensive collection of information, contrasting with the traditional information files in card indexes and folders. Electronic worksheets are used instead of card indexes for the registration of data.

In business use, database programs should be helpful in the management of extensive amounts of all sorts of data. Anyone who frequently works with large quantities of information in card indexes, catalogues or folders will recognize the value of a good database program. There are also many possibilities for application in personal situations, for example, address files or the register of a collection, such as slides, photographs, books or postage stamps.

Programs which deal with data management originated in the world of the large computer system. Due to the fact that personal computers became increasingly more powerful, these devices also became interesting for the database. Moreover, the traditional database systems on large computers cannot fulfil the requirement for information at many (work) locations at once. Databases which are oriented to the personal computer can be applied in a much more flexible way. It is just as easy to

register information in a PC database from the large
computer as to enter it directly at the workplace itself.

Present-day database programs for the personal computer provide the following possibilities:

- defining your own files, geared to the current requirements
- quick and flexible search functions with freely chosen
  search criteria
- easy alteration, deletion and duplication of existing
  records
- formulation of reports in various ways.

In order to be able to work with a database, you must be
familiar with the general structure. The following terms
are important in this context:

field   Each piece of information is entered in a
                field, a data field. Examples of fields in a
                customer file are the name of the com-
                pany, the contact person, the address
                and the telephone number.

record   A record is a group of data which belong
                together, consisting of a number of
                fields. Example: a collection of informa-
                tion about a customer, which could be
                useful to the user.

file   A file is comparable to a card index and
                consists of records which belong
                together. Example: all customer records
                together form a file.

database   A database consists of various files. The
                records of these files can be connected
                to each other using collection criteria in
                such a way that they may be addressed
                through all the files.

12.2   The possibilities of the 1-2-3/W database

In fact, real database management using 1-2-3/W is not possible, it is more a matter of file management. In order to prevent confusion however, we shall regard the terms 'database' and 'file' as being synonymous here.

In 1-2-3/W, working with structured data files takes place using the *Database* command from the *Tools* menu. If you select this command the following submenu appears:

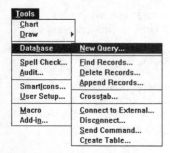

Database submenu

These are the options available:

option	significance
New Query	This option enables you to create a query table by selecting records from a database table.
Find Records	Searches for records which fulfil certain conditions.
Delete Records	Deletes records which fulfil certain conditions.
Append Records	Adds records to a database table.
Crosstab	Makes a cross-tabulation table with data from a database table.

Connect to External	Links a table to an external data-base.
Disconnect	Disconnects the link to the external database.
Send Command	Sends a command to an external database management program.
Create Table	Creates an external database table.

The *Range* menu also contains a number of options which can be used in database management:

option	significance
Fill	Enables you to enter a range of values quickly in a defined range.
Sort	Sorts the rows and records in a table (in ascending or descending order).
Analyze	This option opens a submenu containing diverse commands for database management:

What-if Table
displays in table form the result of the alteration of values in a formula. The table is always recalculated when the value in a formula is altered.

Distribution
analyzes the distribution of values in a range and calculates the frequency.

Regression
performs multiple linear regression analysis of the current data file.

Invert Matrix
the matrices of of rows and columns containing cell data are inverted.

Multiply Matrix
multiplies two ranges as matrices.

The various commands will be discussed below in the light of examples.

12.3   Creating a database in 1-2-3/W

In the following exercise, we shall create a database in
1-2-3/W:

Exercise 12-1: Create a database in 1-2-3/W

In a car firm, a computerized list of second-hand cars
must be installed. Analogous to the card index which
has been in use up until now, the following information
about the second-hand cars must be registered and
managed in a file:

■ make and type
■ amount of HP
■ year of manufacture
■ mileage
■ price.

In 1-2-3/W, a database refers to a worksheet range with
data in a certain structured form, i.e. a system of records and fields. The following rules apply:

■ The record data are registered in a *worksheet row*.
■ Records consist, as mentioned, of various fields. A
  field is displayed in a *worksheet column*.
■ At the beginning of the database, the names of the
  fields must be specified in the first row. This shows
  which sort of information is being dealt with in the
  subsequent data files. It is important not to use the
  same name twice.
■ The actual data are entered in the rows under the
  field names. The contents of each record are related
  to the field name in the first row of the database. The
  records must be entered in the row immediately
  under the field name - there may be no empty rows
  between the field name and the records.
■ In 1-2-3/W, a database may contain a maximum of
  256 fields, due to the fact that a worksheet contains
  no more than 256 columns. Since there are 8192
  rows available, a maximum of 8191 records can be

managed. The first row is reserved for the field names.

12.3.1   Defining and entering fields

In the example, we must first examine the fields to be entered and their names. We shall apply the following names:

- Make
- HP
- Year
- Mileage
- Price.

We shall first begin with a completely new worksheet. The various field names are then entered in the first row of the worksheet. Because all records in a file have the same format, the structure of the record only has to be specified once for each file. Alter the standard column width by specifying the following widths for each column.

Make	20
HP	5
Year	10
Mileage	12
Price	10

The column width is adjusted using the *Column Width* option from the *Style* menu.

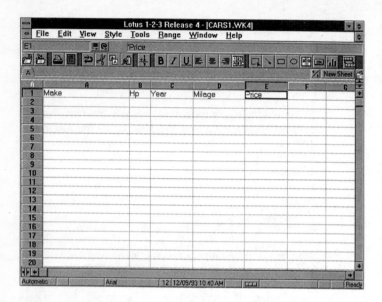

Entering the Field names

When entering data, the following rules must be kept in mind:

■ A text (label) must be specified as the field name. Numbers or formulas are not allowed as field names.
■ A field name may only occur once in a database.
■ Ensure that a field name does not resemble a cell address.

12.3.2   Entering the data

We shall use the following information:

Exercise 12-2: Registering the records

The car firm has a list of second-hand cars for sale.

1   BMW 324 d, 63 HP, Y 1989, ML 22000, Price 19000
2   Ford Fiesta, 55 HP, Y 1988, ML 25000, Price 7000
3   Ford Fiesta, 40 HP, Y 1986, ML 44000, Price 4000
4   Ford Capri, 90 HP, Y 1986, ML 64500, Price 7000
5   Mercedes 190 D, 66 HP, Y 1987, ML 37320, Price
    15000
6   Mercedes 190 E, 90 HP, Y 1988, ML 22000, Price
    17000
7   VW Scirocco, 70 HP, Y 1984, ML 66005, Price 7000
8   VW Scirocco, 110 HP, Y 1988, ML 38000, Price
    14000
9   VW Golf GL, 50 HP, Y 1984, ML 55000, Price 6000
10 Renault R4, 35 HP, Y 1984, ML 63000, Price 3000

In general, the input of records in a database takes place in the same way as the input of data in a normal worksheet. You only need to enter the corresponding data under the field names. Accordingly, place the cell pointer at the first entry field, in this case A2. Subsequently, make the first entry immediately under the name: BMW 324 d. Using the right cursor, confirm the input and move to the next field at the same time. Enter the amount of HP. In this way, the entire record for the first sort can be created. Do the same for all the other sorts.

The result is shown on the following page.

Now save the worksheet with the database under the name SECCAR1 using the *Save As* command from the *File* menu.

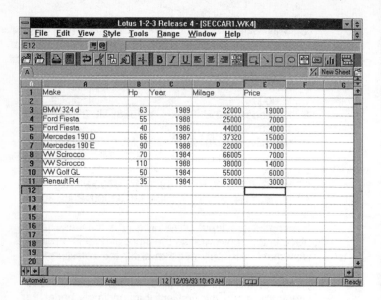

Make	Hp	Year	Milage	Price
BMW 324 d	63	1989	22000	19000
Ford Fiesta	55	1988	25000	7000
Ford Fiesta	40	1986	44000	4000
Mercedes 190 D	66	1987	37320	15000
Mercedes 190 E	90	1988	22000	17000
VW Scirocco	70	1984	66005	7000
VW Scirocco	110	1988	38000	14000
VW Golf GL	50	1984	55000	6000
Renault R4	35	1984	63000	3000

12.4   Finding records

With the 1-2-3/W database, it is possible to look for a particular record so that certain information can be retrieved quickly. We shall illustrate this using the following example:

Exercise 12-3: Finding records

During the course of the day, certain information is requested by interested parties:

(a) Is there a Mercedes 190 D for sale?
(b) Which types of Ford are available?
(c) How many cars have a price tag of less than five thousand pounds?
(d) Is there a Ford Fiesta for less than five thousand pounds?

Records can be sought in 1-2-3/W using the *Database* option from the *Tools* menu. If you open the submenu, the following options will become available:

- searching for records in a database using particular search criteria
- copying records from a database to another part of the database
- searching for specific records
- deleting records from a database.

A precondition of using this menu is that an imput range, a criteria range and, if necessary, an output range are defined.

If you select the *Find Records* command from the *Database* submenu, the following dialog window will appear:

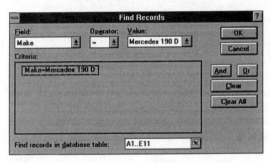

Find Records dialog box

The options in the window have the following significance:

option	significance
Field	Specify here the field for which the search criteria are to apply.
Operator	Specify the operator for the criterion.
Value	Specify in this box the value which the field contents must satisfy.

Criteria	This box displays the result of the criteria you have specified.
Find records in database table	Specify here the location where the search is to take place. It is advisable to specify the database table before activating the dialog box; in that case the box will already contain the required range.
And	This allows you to link selection criteria. The records must then satisfy all named criteria.
Or	Also links selection criteria. The records must fulfil one of the named criteria.

12.4.1   Selecting the database table

The range in a database which is to be edited or in which the search must take place is called the input range. The contents of the input range consist of field names from the database and all entered records which are to be examined.

Prior to being able to carry out a procedure using a database table, you must select it. In our example, that is the range A1..E11.

12.4.2   Selecting fields and records

When you have defined the database table, the criteria which the records must fulfil must be specified. These criteria may refer to one particular field or to a number of different fields in the database. In the latter case, various combinations of the AND and OR operators can be applied to make the search more specific.

In our example, there is a request concerning the availability of a certain make. Therefore, a criterion must be specified for the Make field. When entering selection

criteria in the criteria range, the following rules should
be kept in mind:

■ If a certain text is sought which must conform pre-
   cisely to the criterion, you must specify the exact text.
■ It is also possible to search for a certain value which
   conforms exactly to the specified criterion.
■ A formula can also be a criterion.
■ Various criteria are possible simultaneously.

The dialog window begins with the Field box. The Make
field will be displayed here, but if you wish to specify a
criterion for a different field, open the pull-down menu
and select the required field from the list. The Value
pull-down menu contains the contents of the field. Open
this list and select Mercedes 190 D. You will notice that
the Criteria box now displays Make=Mercedes 190 D.
This is sufficient for the moment; close the dialog box by
pressing Enter or clicking on OK.

The result shows that there is indeed a Mercedes of the
desired type for sale. The record which is found using
the selection criterion is highlighted. Of course, it may
occur that more records fulfil the selection criterion. In
that case, you can use key combinations (see below) to
move to the other records. The program will automatically direct you to the records found, until there are no
more records which satisfy the specified criterion. If you
press Esc or click on a cell, the selection is cancelled.

The following list outlines the significance of the various
keys which can be used to move through the selected
records:

key(combination)   **significance**

Ctrl-Enter   Shows the next record which
                              fulfils the selection criterion.
Ctrl-Shift-Enter   Shows the previous record
                              which fulfils the selection crite-
                              rion.

| Enter | Moves the cell pointer one field to the right within the high-lighted record. |
| Shift-Enter | Moves the cell pointer one field to the left within the highlighted record. |

12.4.3   Special details when selecting records

In the first example, we sought a certain sort of car. For that reason, the label was entered just as it occurs in the database. It is only possible to reach an exact correspondence in that way.

However, it regularly happens that the exact formulation is not precisely known or that texts or values which are located in a certain range have to be found. For these cases, there are special rules. We shall illustrate these using an example. There may be special criteria in the following areas in the car trade:

- Various similar makes have to be found.
- The required car must be within a certain price class.
- The required record must fulfil different criteria.

Comparison of criteria using special characters

The second question in the present example deals with the request for all Ford models. Mark the database table first and then select *Database* from the *Tools* menu. Select *Find Records* from the submenu. The selection criterion is to be 'ford*'. By entering an asterisk, a wild-card is used to represent a longer text. Each random character from the fifth position onwards is assumed to belong to the selection criterion. If you now begin the search procedure, all records will be highlighted in which the Make field begins with Ford.

Special characters can be used in the search procedure.

- The **asterisk** is a wildcard for a longer text.
- The **question mark** is a wildcard for any **one** character.
- A **tilde** (~) in front of the criterion ensures that the criterion is reversed. If the selection criterion is '~ford' for instance, all records which do not contain information concerning 'Ford' will be displayed. This can be a useful criterion, for example, if a buyer arrives who wishes anything but a Ford.

Values and formulas as criterion

Often records are sought which contain certain values or in which the values are located in a certain value range. That is no problem in 1-2-3 /W.

It is possible to formulate selection criteria using certain values. In as much as an exact correspondence with a value is desired, only this value need be specified as the selection criterion in the appropriate cell.

It is different if a conditional correspondence is required. In this case, the selection criterion uses a logical expression as a condition. In this, operators, with which you are already familiar from the spreadsheet, are applied. The formula must be constructed in such a way that a cell address is compared to a random other value.

For instance, if you wish to know which cars cost less than ten thousand pounds, you must enter a formula as the selection criterion for the Price field. The formula is as follows:

```
<10000
```

This criterion <10000 activates the program to find all records with a price of less than ten thousand pounds. Mark the database table and select the command *Tools, Database, Find Records*. For the Field box, specify Price and apply the < sign as the Operator. For

Value, enter the value 10000. The Criteria box now shows:

```
Price<10000
```

Press Enter or click on OK. If everything has gone smoothly, six records will be marked.

Combining criteria

As mentioned, various criteria may be applied at once. We shall examine the possibilities using the following example. In this, two simultaneous criteria must be fulfilled.

Exercise 12.4: Look for all Ford Fiestas costing less than five thousand pounds

Since two criteria have to be satisfied, the criteria must be linked using the #AND# operator.

The procedure is as follows: When you have marked the database table, open the *Find Records* dialog window. Specify for the Make field (in the Value pull-down menu):

```
Ford Fiesta
```

Then click on the And button in order to link this criterion to the next. Now select the Price field, the < Operator and the Value 5000. The specifications are displayed in the Criteria box.

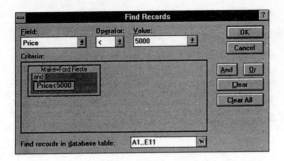

In the example in question, all types of Ford Fiesta which cost less than five thousand pounds will be selected. The result can only be one record, that in row 5.

OR connections are also possible in the database. This concerns records which fulfil one of the criteria. In that case, the different criteria must always be separated by pressing the Or button.

It is also possible to specify compiled logical formulas in one field as a selection criterion. This is necessary, for instance, if more than one condition is to be applied to a certain field. A combination can be made using the operators #AND#, #OR# and #NOT#.

12.4.5   Displaying the search findings separately

We can also transport the result of a search instruction to a separate range of the worksheet. We shall use an example to do this. In this example, we wish to have a list of all cars which are Mercedes or which cost less than ten thousand pounds.

First mark the database table as usual and open the *Database* submenu from the *Tools* menu. Now select *New Query*.The corresponding dialog window appears.

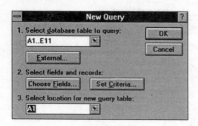

New Query dialog box

Because you have already selected the database table the corresponding range is already shown in the Select Database Table to Query box.

Subsequently, you must specify which fields are to be included in the query table. To do this, activate the Choose Fields button (click on it or press Alt-F). The corresponding dialog box appears. Normally, all fields are registered in the Selected Fields table and if you do not wish them all to be examined, highlight the field which is not necessary and remove it by selecting the Clear button. These field names will be placed above the new Query table in boldface. When you have made your choice, press Enter or click on OK to return to the *New Query* dialog window.

You must now specify the relevant criteria by means of the Set Criteria button. The dialog box which now appears closely resembles that of the *Find Records* dialog window. For Field, select the field to which the criteria are to apply, for Operator select the required operator and for Value specify the value in question. Thus for Make field, specify in the Value box:

```
Mercedes*
```

Then select the Or button in order to ensure that the record only has to fulfil one of the criteria in order to be shown in the output range. Specify the required sum for the Price field.

```
<10000
```

You can check if the criteria have been correctly specified by examining the Criteria box. If this is so, close the
dialog box by activating OK. Now you must define the
output range, in other words, the place where the selected data are to be shown, by entering the required
range in the Select Location for New Query Table box.
You can specify for instance A17. The upper left-hand
corner is sufficient here. You must select an area where
no data are located since the new query table is to be
placed here.

The actual output of the records found by the search
command to the defined range can now begin. This
takes place as soon as you activate OK in the *New
Query* dialog window. The result should be as follows:

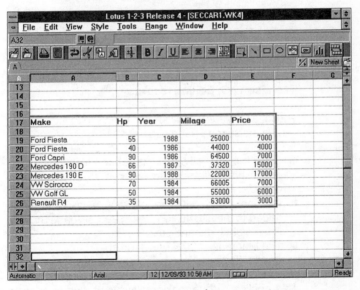

As you see, the records shown consist either of
Mercedes or of cars which are cheaper than ten thousand pounds.

12.4.7   Organizing search commands

If you wish to begin searching in a database all over
again, and you wish to be sure that no data from any
previous commands are unintentionally included, you
should utilize the Clear button in the *Find Records* dialog window if you are working in a database table, or the
corresponding button in the Set Criteria dialog box
when compiling a Query table. In this way you can
remove all criteria specifications in one go.

12.5   Editing Records (file maintenance)

There are various situations in which it is necessary to
alter or update an existing file. It may be necessary to
alter the contents of a record or to delete or add a record.

We shall discuss the possibilities provided by 1-2-3/W
in this area using the following example.

Exercise 12-5: Editing records

The following alterations should be made to the file containing the second-hand cars:

■ Since the 55 HP Ford Fiesta cannot raise the desired
price, this sum must be reduced by one thousand
pounds.
■ An Opel Corsa with the following features must be
added to the file: 45 HP, Year 1990, Mileage 34,000,
Price eight thousand pounds.
■ The Mercedes 190 E has been sold.

In general, records are dealt with as in a spreadsheet.
This applies both to making alterations and to copying
and adding new records.

12.5.1   Altering the contents of a record

In order to make later alterations to the contents of records, you must first go to the appropriate record and select the desired field. You then have the following possibilities:

- You can replace the contents of the field by entering new contents.
- You can alter (edit) the contents after pressing F2.

In the example, proceed as follows to change the price of the Fiesta:

- Using the cursor keys, go to field E4.
- Enter the new price, 6,000.
- Confirm the alteration using Enter.

12.5.2   Adding records

It often occurs that new records have to be included in an existing database.

Exercise 12-6: In our example, a record for the Opel Corsa has to be added along with the following specifications: 45 HP, Year 1990, Mileage 34,000, Price £8000.

Extra records can be inserted or added at any row position in the database:

- Insertion takes place by first creating extra space for the insertion using the *Insert* command from the *Edit* menu. Select Row from the subsequent list of options.
- A record or row can be added to the end of a database without any problem. Keep in mind that any input range for search commands may have to be adjusted.

In our example, the record for the Opel Corsa should be added in row 8. Go to the appropriate row in the database and enter the data concerning the Corsa.

If a group of records are to be added to a database, there is yet another way of adding the records. Select the *Database* option from the *Tools* menu and then choose the *Append Records* command. Subsequently specify an input and an output range as follows. The range from which the new records are to be adopted must be specified in the Append Records From box. The first row of this range must contain exactly the same names as the database table. In the To Database Table, specify the table to which you wish to add the records.

12.5.3 Deleting a record

Obsolete or unnecessary records should be deleted from a database, otherwise the database will no longer be accurate and will become inconveniently lengthy.

For example, when a car is sold, the relevant record can be removed from the database. In our example, this is the case with the record in row 8. Direct deletion of records takes place by means of the *Delete Records* submenu from the *Database* command in the *Tools* menu. The *Delete Records* dialog window appears. In this way, it is possible to delete records which fulfil specified selection criteria. This is especially useful if complete ranges have to be removed in one go.

In the example, the procedure is as follows once the table has been marked and the *Delete Records* option has been chosen:

■ Specify the criterion: Make=Mercedes 190 E.
■ Confirm using Enter or click on OK.

The record will be immediately removed without confirmation from the database table. The remaining records will automatically shift a row upwards.

Save the database again under the name SECCAR2.

Note: Prior to giving a deletion command, it is advisable to use a search command to check whether the correct records will be deleted by means of the specified criteria.

12.6 Analyses using the 1-2-3/W database

An important function of a database is the possibility of executing calculations and analyses. We shall illustrate this using examples.

12.6.1 Distribution analyses in databases

1-2-3/W provides the possibility of calculating the distribution of values in a certain range. This takes place by means of the *Distribution* option from the *Analyze* option in the *Range* menu. The distribution of the different values in the specified range is transposed to a separate worksheet range in which the amount of values which lie between certain numerical limits is shown.

Exercise 12-7: Making a distribution calculation

When planning, it is important to know how the division of the stocks of cars into price class will take place. In the light of a distribution analysis, the amount of cars should be calculated which:

- are cheaper than five thousand pounds;
- cost between five and ten thousand pounds;
- cost between ten and fifteen thousand pounds;
- cost between fifteeen and twenty thousand pounds;
- are more expensive than twenty thousand pounds.

The result is to be stored under the name SEC-CAR3.WK4.

Before the actual calculation can take place, the range in which the results will be located must be defined. In this example, we shall place the results in columns G and H.

Using the cell pointer, go to cell G2 and enter the desired interval values in ascending order in the column. The screen should look like this:

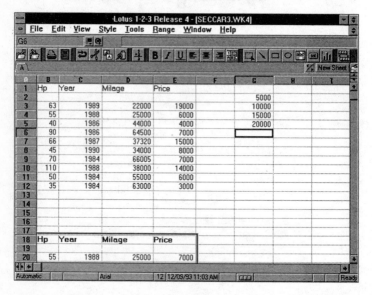

Thus, the interval data are located in the range G2..G5. This range is the left-hand column of the result worksheet and is called the distribution value range. When defining this range, keep in mind that the column to the right must be empty and that there must also be empty cells under the distribution value range.

Now activate the *Analyze* option from the *Range* menu and then the *Distribution* option. Specify the data as described above. You must first specify the range containing the data to be analyzed, in our example that is E3..E12. The interval range (Bin range) is G2..G5. In the analysis only the numerical values are calculated; labels and empty cells are ignored.

The result is as follows:

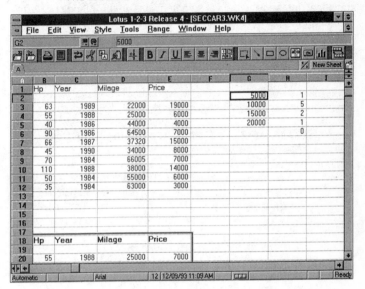

You will observe in the figure that the results of the calculations are placed in the column to the right of the distribution values. You can see how and to what extent the data from the value range fall inside the limits of the diverse intervals. The quantity corresponds to the amount of values in the specified range which is greater than the previous frequency value but is not greater than the actual value (in column G). In addition, the number of values greater than the largest interval value is shown in an extra cell. In our example that is 0 since there is no car costing more than twenty thousand pounds.

The database is saved under the name SECCAR3 using *File, Save*.

12.6.2   Calculations using database functions

It is also possible to calculate average minimum and maximum values in 1-2-3/W. This may be required, for instance, when a selection has taken place, i.e. a request based on certain criteria. At such moments, the statistical functions of the program can be extremely useful.

We shall apply these functions using the following example:

Exercise 12-8: Calculations using statistical database functions

When planning, it can be important to make statistical analyses of a database. Load the SECCAR2 file and examine which makes of car cost more than five thousand pounds. Have the program calculate the following:

- the number of selected values
- the total value of the selected cars
- the average value of the selected cars
- the highest price
- the lowest price

Load the file using the *Open* command from the *File* menu. Mark the database table and select *Tools, Database, Find Records*. For Field select the Price field, for Operator select the greater-than sign and for Value specify 5000. The Criteria box should now display:

```
Price>5000
```

The search will begin when you confirm this by activating OK or pressing Enter.

You can now construct a database range. Increase the column width of H to fifteen characters and enter the text data. The input should take place in the range H2..H6.

H2: Quantity
H3: Total value
H4: Average value
H5: Maximum value
H6: Minimum value

The corresponding formulas must be placed in column
I. Enter the following formula for the quantity of selected
cars:

```
@DCOUNT(A1..E12;"PRICE";Price>5000)
```

Explanation of this formula:

- The first argument between brackets concerns the
  input range of the database. This deals with the field
  names and specified records.
- Subsequently, the field in which the analysis takes
  place must be specified. In our example, this is the
  PRICE field.
- The criterion is specified as the last argument between the brackets. You can also specify the criterion
  elsewhere in the worksheet which means you only
  need to specify here the cell in which the criterion is
  registered.

In the same way, enter the remaining formulas in the
rows 3 to 6 of column I:

```
@DSUM(A1..E12;"PRICE";PRICE>5000)
@DAVG(A1..E12;"PRICE';PRICE>5000)
@DMAX(A1..E12;"PRICE";PRICE>5000)
@DMIN(A1..E12;"PRICE";PRICE>5000)
```

It is, of course, easy to copy these using *Edit, Copy* and
Edit, Paste and to alter the individual formulas using the
Edit (F2) key. You only need to specify the appropriate
function and ensure the range is correct.

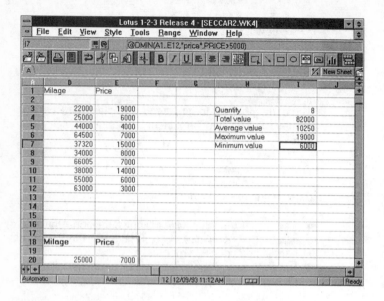

12.7   Sorting records

In principle, records entered in 1-2-3/W are saved in the order of sequence in which they were registered. However, it may be desirable to sort the records in alphabetical or numerical order - for instance, aphabetical according to Make or numerical according to Price.

In 1-2-3/W, this rearrangement takes place using the *Sort* command from the *Range* menu. The *Sort* dialog window is shown on the following page.

In the Sort By text box, specify a cell address in the column containing the data which are to be sorted.

The sorting order can also be determined:

■ Ascending if the sorting is to be done from A to Z or from the largest to the smallest number.
■ Descending if the sorting is to be done from Z to A or from the smallest to the largest number.

Sort window

It is also possible to sort according to additional keys by means of the Add Key button.

The sorting procedure is explained using the following exercise:

Exercise 12-9: Sorting records

The SECCAR2 file containing the information about second-hand cars is to be sorted as follows for calculation purposes:

■ in alphabetical order according to make
■ according to price (most expensive first) within make classification.

Select the database table. In contrast to the previous examples, the row containing the field names (A1..E1) should not be selected; thus this time the range is A3..E12. Select the *Sort* command from the *Range* menu. The *Sort* dialog window appears. For the Sort By field, specify the cell which is to be used as primary sorting key. In our example, this is A1. Activate Ascending for the sorting order. Then click on Add Key.

Then specify the second sorting key in the Sort By box. This is important if there are several records in the field

which are identical in terms of the first sorting key. Now type E1 in the box and activate Descending as the sorting order. Specify the range A3..E12.
Now click on OK to start the sorting procedure. The result is produced immediately and will look like this:

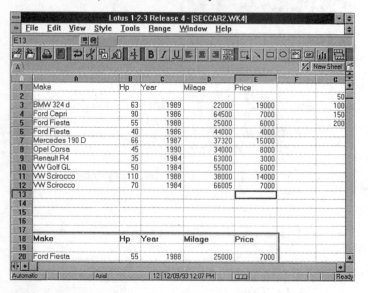

Sorted database

The records are now arranged in such a way that they are presented in ascending order based on the primary sorting key and in descending order according to the secondary sorting key.

Summary of chapter 12

■ Database programs make it possible to manage large amounts or data easily and flexibly. A suitable database structure is a prerequisite for effective use.
■ The options in the *Range* menu and its *Database* submenu enable you to manage data files in 1-2-3/W.
■ The field names should be registered in a worksheet

row at the beginning of a database created under 1-2-3/W. Each name refers to a column.

■ A direct search procedure for information in a database is possible by means of the *Find Records* option from the *Database* submenu of the *Tools* main menu. Before records can be sought, an input range must first be specified. This must contain the field names and the data which is used in the selection.

■ The *Analyze* option from the *Range* menu enables you to execute specific calculations in databases using the Distribution, Regression, Invert Matrix and Multiply Matrix commands.

■ Selection criteria in searches can be texts and values. Question marks and asterisks can also be used as wildcards. Formulas can also be applied as search criteria. They enable you to perform tests according to preconditions.

■ Before a record can be altered, the field which is to be altered has to be activated first. The contents can then be changed immediately. It is also possible to edit the field by pressing the F2 (Edit) key.

■ Records can be removed by means of the *Delete Records* option from the *Database* submenu of *Tools*.

■ Various statistical calculations can be executed in a database by means of the database functions. This can also be done after search commands have been implemented using the *Find Records* command from the *Database* submenu of *Tools*.

■ The *Sort* command from the *Range* menu enables you to sort records into a different order of sequence. Before rearrangement can occur, a data range must be specified containing only the records which are to be sorted. The field names must not be included in this. Several sorting keys may be specified simultaneously.

12.8   Exercises

(1) Create a customer file and enter the following information about the customers:

Cst.nr	Name	Street	PC	Town	Turnover
1742	Twist Ltd.	18 Soho	L17 2AB	London	420,000
2959	Copperfield Ltd.	1 Beech Lane	BA2 3CD	Bath	345,450
6500	Marley Ltd.	2 Rack Road	DV4 5TD	Dover	234,599
4508	Dorrit Ltd.	6 Little Drive	MA5 6OT	Manchester	185,000
1455	Fagin Ltd.	7 Purse St.	L14 3AB	London	80,000
1940	Bumble Ltd.	9 Beadle Ave.	NO2 8EQ	Nottingham	45,000

(2) Specify the relevant criteria for the following applications and subsequently check them:

(a) All customers who live in London.
(b) The address data of Bumble Ltd.
(c) All customer numbers under 4000.
(d) All customers with a turnover of more than
100,000 pounds.

(3) Sort the database according to turnover figures and
save the file under the name CUSTOMRS.

Procedures

(1) Firstly, enter the field names in one row of the worksheet. Each field name requires one column in the
worksheet, making a total of six. Then enter the records one by one, each record in its own row. Proceed as you always do: first go to the desired cell
with the cell pointer, enter the text or value and
move to the next cell using the cursor keys.

(2) Via *Tools, Database, Find Records* a number of selection criteria are to be made.

(a) For Field: Town   for Value: London
(b) For Field: Name   for Value: Bumble
(c) For Field: Cst. nr   for Operator: <
                                     for Value: 4000
(d) For Field: Turnover   for Operator: >
                                     for Value: 100,000

(3) Proceed as follows:

■ Define the range: A3..F8.
■ Open the *Range* menu using Alt-R or the mouse.
■ Select the *Sort* command using S or the mouse.
■ Go to the Sort By text box.
■ Specify the 'Turnover' field by typing F1.
■ Choose the Descending sort order using D.
■ Implement the command using OK.

The last result should be as follows:

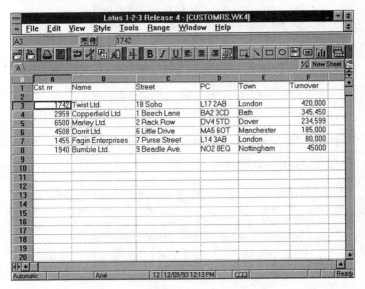

13 Data exchange with other programs

In daily practice, various programs are used simultaneously in many businesses. In addition to spreadsheets, word processors and database programs are commonly in use. Recognizing this fact, 1-2-3/W provides the possibility of exchanging data with other programs.

Data exchange with other Windows programs seldom produces problems. Here we are referring to programs which have been specially designed for Windows, such as AmiPro and Write. Various aspects of this will be outlined in the chapter in the light of examples:

- exchange by means of the Clipboard
- exchange by means of import commands
- dynamic data exchange.

In addition, it is also possible to exchange data with other system environments such as DOS programs. This will also be discussed in this chapter.

13.1 Static data exchange via the Clipboard

The classic method of exchanging data takes place using the Clipboard. This is an electronic buffer in which text and images are stored in such a way that they are available to any other Windows program.

1-2-3/W provides, just like all other Windows applications, the following options in the *Edit* menu:

- Cut
- Copy
- Paste, or Paste Link.

These options enable you to execute all procedures required for exchanging data.

Regardless of the programs between which the data is to be exchanged, the following three steps are necessary to convey data to the Clipboard:

Step 1: Transport to the Clipboard

First you must transport to the Clipboard the table or the section of the table which you wish to use in the target document. To do this, open the source program containing the relevant worksheet and mark the required section. You now have two options to convey this selection to the Clipboard: the *Cut* command and the *Copy* command from the *Edit* menu. If you select *Copy*, the selected area (text, table or chart) remains on the screen. If you select *Cut*, the selection is transported to the Clipboard and simultaneously removed from the screen.

Step 2: Activating the target application

Then activate the target application which is to receive the data in the Clipboard. If the data transport is to an application outside 1-2-3/W, the easiest way of doing this is to use the key combination Ctrl-Esc. In the *Task List* which then appears, switch to the Program Manager in order to start up a different application, for instance the word processor.

Step 3: Adopting the Clipboard contents into the target document

Finally, the data from the Clipboard must be transferred to the activated application. First activate the position in the target document in which the data are to be located. You may then choose one of two options.

■ The *Paste* command from the *Edit* option transports
the data from the Clipboard immediately.
■ If you wish to make a link when carrying out the transfer procedure, you must choose a different command. In that case, you must apply *Paste Link* from
the *Edit* menu. This then means that the data in the
target document will be adjusted automatically when
the data in the source document are modified.

The figure below illustrates the mutual relationship between the applications and the commands:

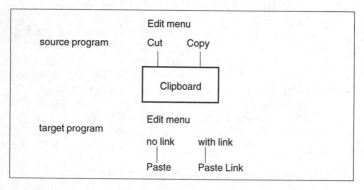

The exchange of data using the Clipboard

Data exchange will be further oulined below in the light
of certain programs and examples.

13.1.1   Data exchange between 1-2-3/W and AmiPro

Data which have been compiled using a spreadsheet
program such as 1-2-3/W are sometimes applied in a
word processor to produce a sales report for instance,
or a quotation. In such cases, the data need not be
typed in a second or third time, they can be adopted
from the source straightaway.

We shall outline an example of how data from 1-2-3/W
can be adopted into AmiPro.

Exercise 13-1: Adopting a 1-2-3/W table into AmiPro

Activate the TURNOVR2.WK4 table created in 1-2-3/W and adopt it into an AmiPro document.

Save the result as TEST1.TOG.

First activate the 1-2-3/W program and open the TUR-NOVR2.WK4 file. Then mark the whole table in the worksheet. Select the *Copy* command from the *Edit* menu. The selected table is stored in the Clipboard.

Now there are various possibilities to activate the target application, AmiPro (assuming that you do have this program):

- Open the system menu by pressing Alt-spacebar or by clicking once on the button in the extreme top left-hand corner. Select the *Switch To* option. Activate Program Manager from the options provided in the subsequent Task List by double clicking on it or by highlighting it and activating Switch To. Then activate the required program in the Program Manager window.

- Activate the Task List using the key combination Ctrl-Esc. Subsequently activate AmiPro by first activating the Program Manager and then selecting AmiPro by double clicking on the icon.

- If you have already activated AmiPro, switch to it by pressing Alt-Tab.

As soon as AmiPro has been started up, write a short report to explain the data. Then move to the position where the 1-2-3/W table is to be inserted. Now open the *Edit* menu and select the *Paste* command. The Clipboard contents are inserted at the current cursor position.

Save the file under the name TEST1.TOG using the *Save* option from the *File* menu.

13.1.2   Data exchange between 1-2-3/W and Write

Similarly, a 1-2-3/W table can be adopted into the Write
for Windows word processing program.

Exercise 13-2: Adopting a 1-2-3/W table into Write using the Clipboard

Adopt the table from the TURNOVR4.WK4 worksheet
into a Write document to produce the following result:

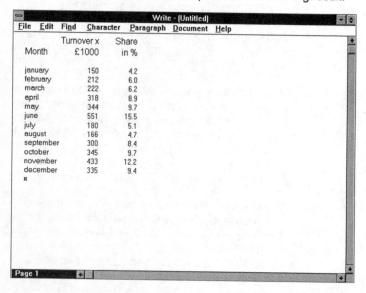

Save the result under the name TEST1.WRI.

Start up the 1-2-3/W program and open the TUR-
NOVR4.WK4 file. Then select the required section from
the worksheet. Now open the *Edit* menu and choose
Copy. The selected table is copied to the Clipboard.

There are now various ways of activating the target application Write.

■ Open the system menu by pressing Alt-spacebar or by clicking once on the top left-hand button on the screen. Select the *Switch To* option. Here select the Program Manager by double clicking on it or by highlighting it and activating Switch To. Now open the required program, Write, in this case. If Write has already been activated, you will be able to start it up directly from the Task List.
■ Activate the Task List by pressing Ctrl-Esc. Then activate the Program Manager and double click on the Write program icon in the relevant group window.
■ If Write has already been started up, switch to it using Alt-Tab.

When Write has been started up, create the document in which the table is to be adopted. Then go to the position where the 1-2-3/W table is to be inserted. Open the *Edit* menu and select *Paste*. The Clipboard contents are inserted at the current cursor position, as you will immediately see on the screen.

13.2   Dynamic data exchange

It is occasionally very convenient, when exchanging data, to create a permanent link between the source file and the target document. In this way, a dynamic method of data exchange, the so-called dynamic data exchange (DDE) is realized.

With DDE, a link between source and target is made:

■ The *target file* is the file which receives the data from another Windows document. Target files may be worksheet files or other Windows applications which support DDE.
■ The *source file* is the file in a Window application which serves as the source of the data. This can be a worksheet or a file from any other Windows application.

As soon as you have made the link, a target file is automatically modified when the data in the (original) source file are changed. The following rules apply:

- If the link is active and automatic adjustment has been specified, each alteration in the source file will be automatically applied to the target file. For example, if you alter a number in the worksheet which functions as the source file, this number will also be adjusted in the target file.
- The link is no longer active when you close the source file. But because the link is saved in the target file, this is restored immediately the source file is opened again.
- When the target file is opened, the link to the saved source file is automatically restored.

We shall explain this process by means of three examples.

13.2.1 Exchange between 1-2-3/W and Write

The adoption of tables from a spreadsheet program into a word processor can be brought about in such a way that the numbers in the text document alter automatically according to any changes which may occur in the integrated table.

Exercise 13-3: Adopting tables with links

In this exercise, the transfer of data from the worksheet to the text is to be realized in such a way that alteration to the source table will automatically be passed on to the text document.

To do this, we shall make use of the TURNOVR4.WK4 worksheet. After the link has been made, we shall change the estimated turnover for January to 777.

Then we shall check if the corresponding value has also been altered in the text document. Save the result as TEST2.WRI.

The result should conform to the figure below:

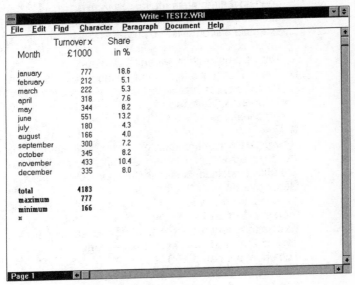

The table adopted into Write after modification in 1-2-3/W

If you wish to make use of the Clipboard in this example, proceed as described previously. The only difference is that you should not select the *Paste* command from the *Edit* menu once you are in Write. Instead, select *Paste Link*.

The procedure is thus as follows:

a) Initial steps in 1-2-3/W:
Activate the TURNOVR4.WK4 worksheet.
Copy the table (section) to the Clipboard using *Edit, Copy.*

b) Switch to another application:
   Activate the Task List by pressing the key combination Ctrl-Esc.
   Activate the required application if it is present in the Task List. If not, activate the Program Manager and start up the required application from there.
   The required application is then opened. In our example, this is the word processing program.

c) Procedures in Write (when started up):
   - type the text or open an existing text
   - move to the insertion position
   - open the *Edit* menu
   - select *Paste Link*.

The tables which are adopted into text documents will be adjusted as soon as the data in the source worksheet are modified. Just to try this out, activate the 1-2-3/W program and change the value of the estimated turnover for January to 777 in the TURNOVR4.WK4 worksheet. In order to examine whether the alteration has actually taken place in the target document, switch over to the word processor. Subsequently save the result under the name TEST2.WRI.

13.2.2   Exchange between 1-2-3/W and Freelance

The dynamic exchange of data not only works with data which are transported from a table to a word processor. It is also possible to integrate charts and images into other documents. This will be demonstrated using the well-known Lotus graphic program *Freelance Graphics*. This program enables you to create various sorts of charts and drawings and to combine them into one presentable object.

Exercise 13-4: Using data from 1-2-3/W for a Freelance image

Imagine that you have created a presentation in Freelance consisting of various images, and this has been saved under the name TECHNO.PRE. An image is now to be placed in this presentation to display data from a 1-2-3/W worksheet, TURNOVR2. The estimated values for the first six months are to be presented as a pie chart. Any later modifications to the worksheet are to be passed on automatically to the Freelance chart.

If you receive the error message that Freelance Graphics cannot read Lotus version 4 files, you will have to save the TURNOVR2.WK4 worksheet as a WK3 file first.

Open the required Freelance presentation file and insert a new image. This is done as follows:

- Open the presentation file.
- Go to the page to contain the chart.
- Select *New* from the *Page* menu.
- Select the first option *Chart*.
- Click on OK to carry out the command.
- Draw the chart area.
- Select Pie as the *Chart Type*.
- Now click on *Import*.
- Select the TURNOVR2.WK3 file and determine the range to be adopted for the labels by marking A4..A9. Click on *Copy Labels*.
- Select the data range (B4..B9) and click on *Copy Data*.
- Now activate the *Link Selections* option by clicking on it. This creates the dynamic data exchange link.

The data have now been recorded in Freelance and you can create the required pie chart in Freelance and edit it further. Save the presentation once more under the name TECHNO.PRE.

Now switch to the 1-2-3/W program using the Task List. Change the value for January to 777. Switch back to

Freelance. The alteration is automatically applied in the chart.

13.2.3 Data exchange between AmiPro and 1-2-3/W

This type of process can also be carried out in reverse. In other words, a 1-2-3/W file can function as the target file. This can be done, for instance, by importing data from a database to create a worksheet, or text from a word processor such as AmiPro. This can be useful if data have been registered using the table function of the word processor.

If you wish to carry out this manoeuvre, first open the source program, in our case AmiPro. Load the file containing the relevant data. Subsequently, mark the section in the document which is to be linked to the worksheet. Select the *Copy* command from the *Edit* menu. The data are now stored in the Windows Clipboard.

Now activate the 1-2-3/W program and open the required worksheet which is to be used as the target file. Activate the target range in the table and select *Paste Link* from the *Edit* menu. The link is created.

Notes:

- Links which have been made can easily be removed again. The link is severed in the target program containing the target file. In 1-2-3/W, choose the *Links* option from the *Edit* menu. Specify the links you wish to remove in the Link Type box. The command is executed by activating the Delete button.
- In the case of a DDE link, it is possible to allow the adjustments to be made either automatically or manually. In order to specify the required setting, select the *Links* option from the *Edit* menu. Click on Edit in the subsequent dialog window. With manual adjustment, you must first select the link which is to be adjusted and then activate the Edit button.

13.3 Data exchange with DOS applications

In practice, you will probably work with both DOS and Windows programs. In that case, it is very convenient if you can also exchange data between these programs. In principle, this is possible by means of the Clipboard. A precondition of data exchange with DOS programs is that the corresponding program also runs under Windows. It is also advisable to have Windows running in the 386 enhanced mode. If not, there are a number of restrictions in the exchange process.

13.3.1 Importing 1-2-3/W tables into DOS applications

Exercise:
Imagine you have created a worksheet in 1-2-3/W and you wish to adopt the data into a text document created in WordPerfect under DOS. We shall try this out using the TURNOVR2.WK4 worksheet (or TURNOVR.WK3 if you receive the error message that the program does not recognize the file format).

WordPerfect 6.0

Type a text in the DOS version 6.0 of WordPerfect. Then select the *Spreadsheet* option from the *Tools* menu. Then choose *Import* to adopt the data in one go, or *Create Link* to enable you to update the spreadsheet data when modifications are made to the spreadsheet. Type, in the Filename entry field, the name of the file you wish to import or link, including the path. Then select the Link & Import option if you wish to create a link, or merely Import if you only wish to adopt the data.

WordPerfect 5.1

Type a text in the DOS version 5.1 of WordPerfect.
Then press Ctrl-F5 and choose Spreadsheet (5).
Choose Create Link (2). Specify the name of the file by
firs: pressing option (1) and then entering the filename.
You can also specify a range if required by means of
option (2). The command is executed when you select
Perform Link (4).

Notes: (for versions 5.1 and 6.0)

■ When specifying a filename, you can use the F5 key
to search for a certain file in a certain directory.
■ If you do not make any further specifications in the
Range option, the entire worksheet will be adopted.

If everything has gone smoothly, the table, along with
the corresponding control codes, will be inserted at the
cursor position. Thus, the table is displayed on the
screen immediately; the so-called control codes are
also present although these are not initially visible (except for the concluding code). You can examine the
codes by pressing the familiar key combination, Alt-F3.
The codes are then shown in the lower half of the
screen. For instance:

```
[Link:A:\TURNOVR2.WK3;<Spreadsheet>;A:A1..A:E14]
[Table def:I;3;1.12";1.12";1.12";1.12";1.12"]
```

13.3.2   Importing data from the DOS versions of 1-2-3

If you have been working with the DOS versions 3.0
and/or 3.1 of Lotus 1-2-3 up until now, data exchange
will be no problem at all. In that case, you only need to
open the *File* menu in 1-2-3/W and select *Open*. Lotus
1-2-3 version 4 for Windows automatically recognizes
the format of the DOS versions.

Appendix
Summary of the commands in Lotus 1-2-3 Version 4 for Windows

File Menu
(file management)

name	function
New	Opens a new, empty worksheet
Open	Activates an existing file
Close	Closes the active window
Save	Saves the current file under its existing name on disk
Save As	Saves the current file under a new name on disk
Protect	Seals the current file and sets file reservation
Send Mail	Sends the current file via electronic mail
Print Preview	Displays the current marked section as it will be reproduced on paper
Page Setup	Regulates page layout
Print	Prints the current selection on the printer
Print Setup	Regulates the printer and printer settings
Exit	Terminates 1-2-3/W

Edit menu
(worksheet editing)

name	function
Undo	Revokes the previous command
Cut	Removes the current marked section and places it in the Clipboard
Copy	Copies the current marked section to the Clipboard
Paste	Imports the current contents of the Clipboard into the worksheet
Clear	Removes the selected data
Paste Special	Defines the way in which the data are to be copied to the cells
Paste Link	Copies and links data so that they are automatically adjusted
Arrange	Opens a submenu for arranging selected charts and drawn objects
Copy Down	Copies the top row of an area to the rest of the area
Copy Right	Copies the most extreme left column of an area to the rest of the area
Insert	Inserts rows, columns or worksheets
Delete	Deletes rows, columns or worksheets
Find & Replace	Finds and replaces text in a selected range
Go To	Goes to the specified location
Insert Object	Inserts data from another application into 1-2-3/W
Links	Creates or modifies links

View menu
(screen options)

name	function
Zoom In	Enlarges the current display by 10%
Zoom Out	Reduces the current display by 10%
Custom - 87%	Restores the default display setting
Freeze Titles	Fixes rows and columns as worksheet titles
Split	Splits the window into two panels or three worksheets
Set View Preferences	Defines the window display

Style menu
(specify data display)

name	function
Number Format	Defines the number format in the current selection
Fonts & Attributes	Defines the text format in the current selection
Lines & Color	Defines the format of query tables or ranges
Alignment	Defines the alignment in a query table or range
Gallery	Formats ranges and collections with one of 14 style templates
Named Style	Defines a cell's style as a named style
Column Width	Specifies the width of the selected columns
Row Height	Specifies the height of the selected rows
Protection	Allows change to cell contents but not to styles when the file is

sealed using File Protect. Sealing a file deactivates the style commands.

Hide	Hides or shows the specified area or worksheet
Page Break	Forces a new page or removes it (both horizontal and vertical)
Worksheet Defaults	Specifies settings for the entire worksheet

Tools menu
(diverse commands for drawing, analysis, macros and add-ins)

name	function
Chart	Creates a chart from the selected data
Draw	Opens a submenu for drawing, for text blocks and for buttons
Database	Opens a submenu for making query tables and working with database tables
Spell Check	Searches for mispelled words or duplications
Audit	Searches for formulas, dependent cells, circular references and links
SmartIcons	Selects an icon set, moves and alters icons
User Setup	Adjusts the 1-2-3/W settings
Macro	Opens a submenu for working with macros
Add-in	Loads or removes an Add-in (companion) program

Range menu
(range functions)

name	function
Version	Opens the Version Manager which controls versions and what-if analyses
Fill	Fills a range with values, dates or times
Fill by Example	Fills a range according to an existing data pattern
Sort	Sorts a range of data
Parse	Converts columns with lengthy labels (from an imported file) to extra columns
Transpose	Copies a range in which columns, rows or worksheets are switched
Name	Assigns a name to a range or removes it
Analyze	Opens a submenu to make analyses and calculate distribution patterns

Window menu
(window display options)

name	function
Tile	Places the opened windows adjacent to one another on the screen
Cascade	Places the opened windows diagonally overlapping on the screen

Help menu
(various help functions)

name	function
Contents	Shows a list of available help topics
Search	Opens a dialog box for specification of the required topic
Using Help	Shows information concerning how to use Help
Keyboard	Shows information concerning key combinations used in 1-2-3/W
How Do I?	Shows information about commonly-used procedures in 1-2-3/W
For Upgraders	Shows information about the new functions in 1-2-3/W and the use of 1-2-3 Classic
Tutorial	Activates the 1-2-3/W tutorial
About 1-2-3	Displays the 1-2-3/W version number and copyright

Chart menu
(this menu appears when a chart has been chosen or the frame defined via *Tools, Chart*)

name	function
Type	Specifies the type of chart
Ranges	Specifies the data ranges to be used in the chart
Headings	Adds titles and footnotes to a chart
Legend	Alters the normal legend provided
Data Labels	Places labels at data points
Grids	Adds or removes gridlines
Axis	Opens a submenu for the specification of axes and scaling
Name	Allocates (different) name to the chart

Set Preferred	Makes the current chart settings the default settings
Use Preferred	Gives the current chart the default style
Numeric Color	Defines a colour or pattern for ranges

Query menu

(options for query tables; this menu only appears when a query table is selected, i.e. a table has been created on the basis of selection criteria via *Tools, Database, New Query*)

name	function
Set Criteria	Sets criteria which determine whether or not a record is included in the query table
Choose Fields	Selects and arranges fields for the query table
Sort	Sorts the data in a query table
Aggregate	Calculates values in a query table with groups of data
Show Field As	Assigns a (different) name to the fields in a query
Name	Assigns a (different) name to the query table
Set Options	Specifies options for working with database and query tables
Show SQL	Shows SQL commands for selecting records in the current query table
Set Database Table	Selects a new database table for the current query table
Join	Performs a query on database tables which have a common field
Update Database Table	Updates the records in a database table according to alterations in the query table
Refresh Now	Immediately updates the records in a query table

Index